ISBN 978-1-331-14448-9
PIBN 10150180

1 MONTH OF
FREE
READING

at
www.ForgottenBooks.com

By purchasing this book you are eligible for one month membership to ForgottenBooks.com, giving you unlimited access to our entire collection of over 1,000,000 titles via our web site and mobile apps.

To claim your free month visit: www.forgottenbooks.com/free150180

English
Français
Deutsche
Italiano
Español
Português

www.forgottenbooks.com

Mythology Photography **Fiction**
Fishing Christianity **Art** Cooking
Essays Buddhism Freemasonry
Medicine **Biology** Music **Ancient
Egypt** Evolution Carpentry Physics
Dance Geology **Mathematics** Fitness
Shakespeare **Folklore** Yoga Marketing
Confidence Immortality Biographies
Poetry **Psychology** Witchcraft
Electronics Chemistry History **Law**
Accounting **Philosophy** Anthropology
Alchemy Drama Quantum Mechanics
Atheism Sexual Health **Ancient History**
Entrepreneurship Languages Sport
Paleontology Needlework Islam
Metaphysics Investment Archaeology
Parenting Statistics Criminology
Motivational

MONTH

IN THE

CAMP BEFORE SEBASTOPOL.

LONDON.
A. and G. A. SPOTTISWOODE,
New-street-Square.

MONTH

IN THE

CAMP BEFORE SEBASTOPOL.

BY A NON-COMBATANT.

H. A. Blackburn

SECOND EDITION.

LONDON:

LONGMAN, BROWN, GREEN, AND LONGMANS.

1855.

CONTENTS.

LETTER I.

LETTER II.

LETTER III.

A MONTH

IN THE

CAMP BEFORE SEBASTOPOL.

LETTER I.

Off Malta, Sept. 24th.

So you do not altogether approve of my pro-
ject of passing a few weeks in the Crimea, and
are inclined to think I shall be " in the way ?"
I confess I cannot quite make out from your
letter how this is to happen.   Surely the Seat
of War is a large enough place for all the
people now in it, and many more, to live
and walk about in, without jostling ?   I carry
my own house and commissariat with me.
You do not expect me — do you — to pester
the Generals with morning calls, or to play the
Boy Jones at their councils ?

For my own part, I see no other satisfactory
mode of finding out what our gallant fellows
are really doing and suffering, than by pitching

B

one's tent among them.　Their own letters, deeply interesting as they are, do not supply all the information that is wanted.　Soldiers write like soldiers; that is to say, a kind of professional stoicism restrains them from describing one half of what they go through, while habit dulls their consciousness of the other.　Even "Our Own Correspondent," who now-a-days does such excellent service in this respect, leaves something to be desired.　He is obliged to be so clever, so busied with the depths and general bearings of things about him, that he cannot fail to leave many gleanings for a plain man to pick up.　In short, I am already half-way to my goal; and by the time you are reading this apology for my journey, I hope to be seeing History.

Let me now ask, whether you happen to want a good mental alterative after Nisi Prius?　If so, pray select, either for yourself or a friend, a kit for the Crimea.　You will go, of course, in the first place, to Edgington's warehouse across London Bridge; where you will choose a tent with a view to the various incidents which you think, on reflection, may be looked for at the Seat of War.

You will, next, lay in your commissariat and special clothing; your canteen, your saddle, pack-saddle, and saddle-bags : lastly (for, however comical, it must be done), you will provide against Cossacks with a revolver! All this, of course, cannot be effected in a day; and many books and friends will have been consulted, to enable you to make a proper selection. But, by the time it is accomplished, I venture to predict that you will have gone through a complete campaign in imagination, and will have experienced as many sensations as if you had made the Grand Tour in person. At any rate, I don't envy the clients who may consult you during the process. So exciting, I confess, did I find this kind of vivid projection of myself into a totally strange sphere, that there came, at length, a moment of reaction, when I felt that I had sufficiently realised the incidents before me, and that the actual execution of my plan would be—a bore! Were you never guilty—of course, in thought only, and for the shortest possible time—of a similar absurdity, *amico mio?* However, *that* soon passed; and, piling up my traps upon two cabs, on the 13th of September,

I found myself, by nightfall, not in the least
sick, and already out of the Mersey.

Thus far we have journeyed prosperously
enough — no storms, hurricanes, or any other
of the catastrophes which make a voyage
amusing to the impartial reader. But you,
who are so much occupied with " the Eastern
question," may be interested in learning, that
we carry with us no less than twenty Polish
volunteers for the Turkish army. They came
on board, with a letter of introduction to the
Captain from Lord Dudley Stuart; and are
destined for a cavalry corps in course of
formation, which, together with two others
already embodied, will complete Sadik Pasha's
brigade. That chief, as perhaps you know,
is himself a Pole; his more Christian de-
nomination being Michel Chaikowsky. The
brigade goes by the name of " The *Turkish*
Cossacks "— a title adopted, according to our
volunteers, out of deference to Austria, who,
they declare, objects to the more natural
epithet. Certainly, a Pole by any other name
will hit as hard ; and they are right not to
stick at a trifle. But you will agree that a
simpler explanation is to be found in the fact,

that Poles form an insignificant minority in the brigade. Major ——, than whom there can be no better authority on such a point, told me he himself saw them, not long ago, manœuvring at a review, on scraggy ponies, and at a foot's pace; and that the only men worth their salt among the number (not excepting the Pasha) were veritable Cossacks—inhabitants of a colony planted in Turkey many years back, under the auspices of Catherine the Naughty.

Au reste, our adventurers are mild, mustachioed, musical men — equal, nevertheless, to a stroke of trade when occasion serves. Thus, they were provided with first-class passages—at the expense, I presume, of other pockets than their own. Hearing, however, on our arrival at Gibraltar, that there were more applications for first-class berths than could be granted, their gallant leader quietly proposed to the Captain, on behalf of himself and his friends, that they should finish the voyage as second-class passengers, on " a consideration" being given them for the sacrifice. The offer was, of course, declined; but it proves them to be smart Officers—if in no other sense — within the Yankee meaning of the term.

I shall post this at Malta, where we arrived to-day. Know'st thou the land of the Orange and Mitten (I allude to the blood-red and black-lace varieties respectively) — *kenns't du es wohl?* Then you won't be surprised to hear, that I look forward to leaving it to-morrow without regret. Know'st thou it not? Then learn that it is a Peter Schlemhil of a place, with no shade, save in the faces of the natives; while these are so plain, that the eye is fain to revert to the glare. Fancy an island which looks as if it had been deluged with a rain of light ochre, reducing town and country, soil, pavement, and roofs, to a uniform yellow; banish trees and grass from the landscape; place the whole under a blinding sun; and, with your mental optics, you will gaze, or rather blink, at Malta. Hurrah, therefore, for the cool blue sea again to-morrow!

Hitherto, the mere aspects of sky and ocean have been enough for my enjoyment. After all, it was something to escape, at a bound, from a country where the best part of people's " sensations " reach them through the medium of small pica, to the wild Atlantic —something for a busy man to plunge at once into a mode of existence where the mere perceptions, though confined to a few simple combinations of air, light, and water, are yet vivid enough to dispense with reflection, and where one can live through one's eyes, like a child. How long would it not take to weary of a sky, which, at mid-day, glows with the hue of the turquoise; growing fainter from the zenith, till, at the horizon, it shows like pearly-white against a tumbling ocean of lapis-lazuli? How long, before one would tire of tracing the long eddies of foam which, whirled below the surface in the vessel's wake, curl away, like wreaths of pale green mist, through the blue abyss? How long might not one be content to lie o' nights on deck, in this soft warm air, watching the stars as they reel around the rocking masts; while, swelling above the bulwarks, the phosphorescent waves might almost make you dream, that you were rushing through some mazy dance of meteors, in which the heavens and sea were commingling? How long? Why, we are both of us yawning—so, perhaps, such enjoyments have their period. Never mind; my next will be dated from *terra firma:* on the 1st, we expect to land in Turkey.

LETTER II.

Black Sea, Oct. 3rd.

I TRUST you are prepared to make a very rapid transit with me to Constantinople. The shores of the Ægean and the Hellespont, with all their glories, are they not written in the Handbooks of Murray? And is not one great end of those rubicund tomes even this —to shame garrulous travellers out of describing what has been well enough described already? The fact is, it is not the time of year for such places. The "Isles of Greece," in September, are a cluster of brown rocks; and the most interesting fact I have to record about them is, that, at Syra, an Austrian lady became our fellow passenger, attended by a lively little Greek brunette, who, with hair disposed in the true "Zoe" style, and feet guiltless of shoes and stockings, had, withal, those soft, playful, innocent eyes—which do so much mischief on board ship. She bore the classical name of Πολλυδία. Modern Greeks, you know, pronounce υ like *y*, and care much more for accent than quantity; so be pleased to call her—no, not *Polly dear!*—but *Pollýdia.*

As regards Besika Bay, with the plains of
Troy, and Ida, in the background—our pace
was too good for any effect, save that of
shaking my faith in the applicability of the
epithet " woody" to the mountain in question.   Summer, one is bound to believe, must
make a great difference, or Homer would
never have peopled so bare and palpable a
height with gods and goddesses.   Be that as
it may, the story of Old Troy and The Battle
of the Ships bid fair to outlast the memory
of our fleet in the same regions, unless this,
too, can contrive to get embalmed in some
poetical lie.

The sun shone brightly as we steamed by
the castles of Europe and Asia, which reflected
his rays from batteries resplendent with fresh
whitewash ; not so, alas ! as we rounded
Seraglio Point, where a fog, worthy of London,
made the Bosphorus as dingy as the Thames.

It was ten o'clock on the morning of the 30th
September; we had anchored within the Golden
Horn; your humble servant was growling at
the ill-timed mist; and his companions were
duly telling over the historical rosary by the
Guide Book for that place made and provided;

when a barge, full of red-fezzed, loose-trousered soldiers, was rowed by. " Look at those lazy Turks," cried somebody. " Those are not Turks," said a gentleman who had just come up the ship's side ; " they are *Zouaves*, wounded at the Alma :" and in a moment, he was telling us the glorious tale ! I leave you to imagine the effect of such a recital in such a scene. There, with her rich argosies, her full-domed mosques, and spear-like minarets, lay Stamboul, coveted of Czars —

.   .   . " teterrima belli Causa."

Yet no one thought of her. Every eye was fixed on the narrator, or followed the receding forms of those who had bled in the conflict he was describing ; while the faces of the listeners burned as if they already felt the breath of War. For myself, two facts soon absorbed my faculties. One was, that the transport " Cambria " was to start for the Crimea next morning ; the other, that Admiral Boxer had the giving away of the passages. I hurried to the office, and was successful. So vanished one at least of the lions which fearful friends had descried in my path.

The next morning saw me and my servant, tents and baggage, *en route* for Balaklava, and steaming past Scutari barracks. The latter, as you know, are now used as a hospital; and I hear that so many of the rooms are occupied by wounded Russians, that some of our countrymen are lying in the passages !

It has a strange effect, this thickening of the incidents of war around one. The very transport in which we are now travelling, carried, a fortnight ago, 400 men sick with cholera, smallpox, and fever, to Scutari. There were four doctors on board, who worked like slaves day and night; but, as they could not perform miracles, and had only arrow-root and brandy to administer, their patients died in crowds. The cabins have since been fumigated with gunpowder, and squibs, and chloride of lime — not enough so, however, to quiet the suspicions of a transport captain, who is our fellow-passenger, and who persists in making his nights miserable in the saloon. This comes of being too knowing: the odds are, that he will sicken on his precautions.

At Buyukdereh, a detachment of the 1st

(Royal) dragoons came on board, after being very nearly wrecked in a sailing transport. The tug which had towed them from Varna, had abandoned them from stress of weather. Ere long, the guns of the vessel got unlimbered in the storm, and a beam, to which the horses were tied, fell and crushed crowds of the poor creatures beneath it. One (a fine mare) leapt overboard; others were shot, by the violence of the motion, into the hold; others, from terror, struggled so convulsively, that they were dangerous to approach; while the rest, with eyes knocked out, and bones protruding from their skin, were dashed from side to side on the deck at each roll of the vessel; and the only wonder is, that they and the un-limbered guns, between them, did not stave in the bulwarks, and send the whole affair to the bottom. The second day, proving a little less rough, was passed in throwing overboard the dead horses, which had begun to stink almost immediately — the lurches of the ship being taken advantage of for that purpose — and, in the evening, she reached Buyukdereh. During all these hours of uproar and dismay, no human lives were sacrificed. Still, 100 animals perished in the storm — a very great loss to the service at this time; and a yet greater one to the Officers, who each possessed two or three nags, worth from 100*l*. to 150*l*. a-piece; for not one of which will the frugal public pay more than 30*l*. or 40*l*. compensation.

Two such days and nights would hardly tend, you might suppose, to sweeten men's tempers; yet nothing can exceed the good humour and pleasantness of the new comers. Since their arrival, moreover, our evenings have been enlivened with music. Three or four troopers who, in peace-time, belonged to the Band, play tunes on their bugles, varied by songs from those who possess vocal qualifications. I wish you could see one of these moonlight concerts. The men come out in every variety of dress and undress — some with the brass helmet on; some wearing over it the white linen cover, with loose side-flaps; others with their heads tied up in red handkerchiefs, their tall figures wrapped in military cloaks, or, yet more picturesquely, draped in blankets. The Officers gather near, on the poop, and join heartily in the plaudits; but it is a point of etiquette for the men to ignore their presence. Presently a song is called for; and a huge mustachioed giant advances to the window of the steward's cabin, and clears his voice. He is the *gran tenore* of the regiment. Standing outside the cabin, and placing his hands on the roof, about as easily as you might rest yours on a mantelpiece—the light falling full on his face—he sings some Tyrtæan strain, darkly alluding to the Czar, under threats of "driving back to his mountains the grizzly old Bear;" and each verse closing with the refrain—

"Then cóme along —cóme along — drink while you may
To-morrow we fight, boys (*bis*) — let's be happy to-day!"

Poor fellows! The chorus is real enough for them; and the monotone of the rushing water as the ship dashes on with them to her Goal, does not lessen its significance. But the concert is soon over, as our hours on board ship are early. So, good night!

LETTER III.

Camp, Oct. 6th.

THE bold headlands of the Crimea loomed on our horizon on the afternoon of the 3rd; and we anchored in Eupatoria Bay just in time to hear the bells on board some twenty great black men-of-war announce midnight. Here we learnt — what we were unpatriotic enough to hail as good news — that Sebastopol had yet to be taken. At dawn, we resumed our voyage, and a fine day showed to great advantage the bluff, scarped masses of the interior. Every second mountain seemed a natural fortress; it was like passing a series of Gibraltars.

Sebastopol we reconnoitred at a respectful distance. A jet of light smoke leapt every now and then from the forts, but at too long intervals to make us apprehensive that the assault was in progress. In less than an hour more, we were steaming straight into what seemed a curved bank of high lime-stone rocks. It soon proved, however, to be obliquely cut, about the centre, by a narrow inlet, like the estuary of a second-class river.

Balaklava harbour (for such it was) is nothing
more than the continuation below the sea's
level of a precipitous gorge. For some distance from its mouth, it may be said to be
skirted less with shores than with walls; and
so rapidly do these descend, that within a few
feet of them ride our men-of-war, lying side
by side, as snug as if in dock.

Our first introduction to Enemy's Country,
will never, I am sure, be forgotten by any
one of our party who was gifted with a sense
of the noisome. At the entrance of the harbour, considerable curiosity had been excited
on board by the spectacle of a dead horse, its
legs sticking starkly out of water, being towed
by a steamer out to sea. But the reason soon became obvious to the dullest olfactories. Floating
in all directions, but especially near shore, were
the bloated bodies and fragments of animals,
in every stage of decomposition, and in numbers sufficient to account for quite as much
sickness as we afterwards heard was in the
place. I suppose it can't be helped; but " 'tis
pity;" because here are maintained two hospitals for the poor fellows from camp. As regards
our own party, you may be certain no one among

us was going to play Hotspur's "waiting gen-
tlewoman" thus early in the day. So, gaily
ignoring the carrion, we here wished each
other good speed, and went our several ways.

Fortunately for me the —— was in harbour. Next morning, therefore (having
slept on board the transport), I set off to
deliver my letter and parcel. I found
that —— was closeted with Lord Raglan;
and, waiting till he was disengaged, I employed the interval in observing the scene
around me. The town, though it boasts one
or two mean-looking churches, and though a
ruined tower crowns one of the heights above
it, is a sad tumble-down affair. It is situated
two or three hundred yards from the mouth
of the harbour, and straggles for about a
quarter of a mile along the South side of it, on
the narrow strip of shore which there inter-
venes between the water and the rock. In
general effect, it reminded me of the sort of
places one sees in some parts of Ireland, where
stone is abundant, and nothing else; and
where copious whitewash does duty for repairs.

Lord Raglan's house was not much
above the level of the general wretchedness.

C

Before the door paced to and fro a sentry,
whose get-up was not at all out of keeping with his situation.   He had a soiled
red coat; its ragged worsted tags were the
reverse of ornamental; and its open collar
showed neither stock nor shirt.   His rusty
black trousers gaped vainly here and there
for buttons, and were tucked up unceremoni-
ously at the heels to keep dry.   His boots were
the colour of the dust they trod on; so were
his Saxon locks, and sunburnt face.   Nevertheless, there was that about his quiet honest
bearing which would, I think, have proclaimed
him,   even   without   the   distinctive   red,   a
British soldier.

The quay before the house was one struggling
mass of bullock-waggons, dromedaries, and am-
munition-carts.   There were Jack-tars in couples
baling out of barges heavy shot, and using
for that purpose an iron instrument, shaped
like two Greek ss placed over each other, one
upside down, and the other erect, so that the
circles coincide (each man takes hold of the
two prongs at his own end, and the shot lies
in the central ring).   Commissaries were shouting to bombardiers, soldiers were imprecating

araba-drivers, who in their turn were taking a vicarious vengeance by prodding their beasts. But that the whole business was not so chaotic as it looked, was proved by the continuous line of carts, full of provisions and munitions of war, which streamed steadily off towards the camp.

While I was watching this novel scene, —— came out into the porch, and most hospitably invited me to make the —— my head-quarters during my stay in the Crimea. Upon my expressing, however, a desire to reach the front without delay, he, with equally ready kindness, gave me the means of doing so. I now returned to the "Cambria" for my baggage, and found her already invaded by a tattered, but gallant, troop from the camp. They had cleaned out pretty nearly everything; but I succeeded in buying a bottle of whiskey (5s.), two live ducks, a ham and tongue (all for moderate prices), and a lump of salt. The last luxury I was put up to purchasing by one of the new comers, who gave me many good hints on the subject of my commissariat. I don't know my benefactor's name, but sure I am that he was an accomplished forager and excellent man.

Leaving my baggage to follow with my servant, I set off to the camp, and was lucky enough
to get a lift in an araba, which was conveying
a sick Officer to the same Division of the Army
as that to which I was destined. "Luck," you
know, is a comparative word. The vehicle in
question was simply a basket on wheels,
drawn by bullocks, and devoid of springs,
cushions, seats, or any other contrivance
for saving the human vertebræ from dislo-
cation. The driver was one of a batch of
Crim-Tartars, who were pounced upon — bullocks, waggons and all — by our troops, on
their march to their present quarters.

As matters turned out, I had plenty of leisure
to philosophise on the features of this specimen
of the human race, which did not strike me as
very Mongolian in type. His cheek bones, like
those of many others of his brethren whom I
have since observed, were not particularly
high ; his eyebrows did not slope up, as I had
expected, _à la Chinoise ;_ nor was his mouth
of any remarkable amplitude. The chief
peculiarity about the Crim-Tartars lies, I
think, in their nose, which, though straight,
is so small, both as to length and prominence,

that, set as it is on a full round face but slightly garnished with beard, it gives them the appearance of overgrown boys. Although prisoners, they look fat and jolly enough; and have, indeed, small cause to look otherwise; seeing that we pay them 5*l.* a month, out of which, I hear, they manage to save money.

Just as we had commenced jolting along at the bottom of our basket, my friend ——, who is one of General ——'s Aide-de-camps, happened by good luck to cross our path. His face had got so gloriously blowzed, and he sported so magnificent a beard, that nothing but the tones of his hearty voice enabled me to recognise him. After a brief welcome, he galloped off to give directions as to the pitching of my tents; and I jogged on my way, rejoicing at having come thus early across his cheerful presence.

But hour after hour passed; the distance was only six miles; we had mounted many hills, and fathomed many ruts — yet no camp was visible. The sun, moreover, was setting, and we were in enemy's country. Above all, our compound contusions were beginning to tell. Fiercely turning, therefore, on the arabajee, we charged

him with the design of taking us to Sebastopol!
Perhaps, the accusation was true; most probably, it was not: certain it is, that, after an
animated discussion, in which "Johnny"
(equivalent to *heark'ye!*), in connection with
"Bono" and "No Bono," formed pretty nearly
the only language common to all parties,
our Jehu turned bolt round, took a direction
at right angles to that which he had been pur-
suing, and brought us, a little after dark,
within sight of the camp-fires of the ——
Division.

And now, should you ever run your head
against the "Great Asian Mystery," and have
to discourse on the marvellous virtues of the
Arab race, set it roundly down, that they
are hospitable because they live in tents.
Under similar conditions of canvass, John
Bull beats them hollow! Such, at least, was
the ethnological conviction — the more valuable, as I never travelled in Arabia — which
flashed across me on arriving at the ——
Division. My traps had not come up; I
was an idler in the midst of stern work; yet
not only did my friend —— invite me for
that night to share his pavilion (it is 6 feet
long, by 3 high, and 2½ broad), but General

——, to whom I merely carried a letter of introduction, pressed me most kindly to accept a corner of his, and that, though one of his Aide-de-camps already divides it with him.

While it was yet uncertain whether I should have to close with either of these good-natured offers, dinner was served, and I became a hungry partaker. The appetite inspired by my long drive did not prevent my looking with considerable interest at the novel *entourage* of this my first camp-repast. The General's tent differs in no respect from those of the common soldiers. A single wax-candle, placed on the ground, lit the interior. Canvass forage-bags, cloaks, and waterproofs, spread around, hid the bare earth; and on them reclined, *more antiquo*, the General and his Staff. I alone enjoyed the dignity of a seat, viz., a portmanteau. No such thing as table, chair, bed, bedding, or couch, was visible. As I looked at these simple arrangements, I could not help thinking—if such was all the comfort enjoyed by a General in the Crimea, what must be the condition of inferior Officers? It was not till afterwards that I learnt that, in these

respects, Sir —— —— cannot be persuaded
to allow himself, either on the score of his years
or of his rank, the smallest advantage over his
subalterns.   Fortunately, however, for my un-
Spartan appetite on the occasion in question, it
does happen that the General, having to feed
three lusty Aides, keeps a French *chef;* and this
incomparable artist, though he cooks *al fresco,*
is said to be capable of doing anything short
of transmuting ration-pork and biscuits into
soles au gratin.   A very good dinner was
followed by coffee, and by tobacco for the
juniors.

You do not, of course, imagine that our
entertainment was of the full-dress order.
Everybody, in fact, except my unmilitary
self, wore the working Staff-uniform — blue
frock and gilt buttons, blue red-striped
trousers, and high boots — nor did any one
doff his gold-laced forage-cap, in compliment
either to the occasion, or to the flimsy
canopy which alone protected our heads
from heaven.   Altogether — setting aside a
certain grotesque figure on a portmanteau
— a painter might have made something of

the gallant group which, lit by that solitary candle, lay, little dreaming of a tableau, round the person of their chief.

Meantime, my tents had arrived, and I retired to assist in pitching them. The campfires had all gone out; but there, sure enough, by the light of the stars, appeared a small heap of bags and portmanteaus, shot out on the bare earth; out of which (it required a strong effort of reason to believe) I was thenceforth to find myself in bed, board, and lodging. The tents were soon out of their bags, and sprawling over the ground. But how to put them up? My servant, John Economites — a native of the Ionian Islands, whom I had engaged at Constantinople — had never done such a thing in his life. My friend ——'s camp-servants, on the other hand, were only accustomed to the Regulation bell-tents, from which mine differed considerably. Moreover, the night was cold. It was decided, under these circumstances, that, leaving the more recondite portions to be put up next morning, we should confine our attention to the outer wall of the principal tent; and this, after a vigorous effort of our united intellects, we succeeded in erecting properly. My traps were soon placed inside; a water-proof blanket, 'ycleped a "waterdeck," spread out on the ground, served for a bed; and, with the unattached canvass tent-lining for bed-clothes, I made no doubt that I should pass the night comfortably (N.B. Nobody undresses in camp, except for ablutionary purposes). My friend ——'s servant engaged to find lodging for John. The only other living beings remaining to be provided for, were my two ducks, which were hung up by the heels to one of the strings from the roof of my tent. With a parting counsel not to be disturbed if I heard a little musketry before dawn — that being the favourite time for the Cossacks to vex our pickets — my friend wished me good-night.

I was soon asleep; when, hark! what sound was that close to my ear! Cossacks? then Cossacks must make very singular noises! "Quack-quack, quack-quack, quack-quack!" At last, thoroughly awake, I remembered the suspended ducks. Poor creatures—I reflected—

they are certainly addicted, when at liberty on
the water, to thrusting their tails up and their
heads down.; but, perhaps, so prolonged an in-
version of the centre of gravity as they had
now undergone, might have become a little
too much of a good thing. So, emerging
most reluctantly from my warm nest, I
placed them (merely tying them together
by the feet to prevent escape), on the ground,
and went to sleep again. In vain! Once
more the wretched couple — may-be, grown
sick of each other — set up their confounded
clamour; and this time so loudly, that I
thought ——, his brother Aides, and the General himself, would be awakened by it! The
case evidently called for extreme measures.
Moodily lighting my candle, therefore, and
gazing awhile at the doomed pair, I sought
among the litter around me for an imple-
ment suitable to the crisis — that night they
quacked no more!

It was not long before my rest was
broken, as —— had predicted, by distant
musketry. In another minute, I could hear
the prophet, in his proper person, ordered off

to ascertain the cause. Away went his horse's hoofs in the direction of the firing; whence, after a few minutes, they as quickly clattered back to the General. " Fall in!" —"Get under arms!" now buzzed along the lines; followed by a heavy trampling of feet, as the men ran from their tents to their firelocks. I had been forewarned that these "alarms" were constant, and had nothing necessarily alarming about them; but, being dressed and booted, I could not resist going out to see what was doing. There, in their grey great coats, and already formed in line, stood the soldiers of the —— Division. Three minutes before, they were in dream-land. The musketry had ceased, but no more sleep was in store for them that morning. The " alarm " had, in fact, occasioned a turn-out half an hour before the period (four A. M. till sunrise) consi-dered to be the most likely for attempts at sur-prises; and which is, therefore, in obedience to a Standing Order, always passed under arms. It was now bright moonlight and bitterly cold. So, shivering both for myself and them, I ran back under cover, and dived under the pile

of lining — feeling, I confess, a good deal like
a Sybarite, who has no business to be so com-
fortable.   Nevertheless — but that, you'll say,
only completes the resemblance — I soon slept,
and soundly; till daylight, and a buzz of con-
versation, of which my woven walls gave me
the full benefit, banished all further ideas of
repose.

LETTER IV.

IT certainly has a strange effect, to awake from some dream of England to midnight in camp ; to stretch out one's hand in sleep against the dew-drenched canvass, and suddenly become conscious, that you are *on the Czar's land without leave.* It takes a moment or two to remember, that the perfect stillness is not solitude; that the slumbering host around is encircled by hundreds of wakeful eyes ; and that a single shot, a single cry, would send a shock of life through the whole mass!

That is to say, the effect *did* strike me as strange. But I have now been under canvass four days, and am grown so familiar with a hundred equally strange things, that I see clearly, if I do not at once attempt to give you some notion of them, I shall become as incapable of doing so, as if I had been out here for a twelvemonth.

Whatever intricate dogmas may prevail on the subject, there can be no doubt that human happiness, in some situations, depends largely on a man's kit. Mine is whimsically said to be a luxurious one; so it may the better serve to suggest the state of other people's. Some idea on this subject you must perforce have, before I can explain to you the character of a day in camp.

Let us begin, then, with my domicile. It is one of Benjamin Edgington's "Travellers' Tents," and differs altogether from the Regulation "bell-tent" of the Army. The latter—as you probably are aware—is composed of a cone about eight feet high, with a diameter of fourteen, on a circular wall a foot and a half high; the whole supported by a single pole. The shape of mine is that of two oblong planes inclined against each other, with their bases (which are twelve feet long) about ten feet apart. It is supported by three very light poles, which take to pieces. The centre one is about eight feet high; the two at the ends are two feet shorter; so as to give the top line of the roof a slightly pyramidical character. The perpendicular walls at the two ends are bisected from top to bottom, and the halves can either be reefed up, so as to leave an open entrance; or they can be laced together, when they effectually shut out the wind.

This shape, which, I believe, obtained for its inventor a reward at the Great Exhibition, has certainly some advantages over the bell-tent. Being less tall and more compact, it does not, in a gale, make such a deafening rattle — and that, by the way, is no slight consideration in a camp, where a quick ear when one is *in* one's tent, is as important as a quick eye when one is *out* of it. Again, in hot weather, by reefing the doors at the two ends, you can obtain a draught through the whole tent from top to bottom; whereas in the other, where there is but one entrance through a little flap in the side, a draught can only be made by reefing the circular wall; and as this is only a foot and a half high, the current scarcely reaches a man on a camp-bedstead, while the hot air in the body of the tent remains quite unagitated.

The only inconvenience I have discovered in the shape of the "Traveller's Tent," is one that would not affect travellers in general; and for aught I know, even it might be remedied. There are two ropes attached to the tops of the poles at each end, which require to be pegged down on the ground, at a distance of from five to six feet fore and aft of the tent. As the bell-tents are otherwise constructed, nobody in camp looks out for these projecting supports; and at night, especially, they are sad stumbling-blocks. In fact, a horseman has just given the tent so violent a shock through this cause, that my unfortunate aneroid has been precipitated from its nail on the centre pole, and will never foretell weather more.

But the grand comfort, or as they call it here, the "luxury" of my tent, is one that is independent of its external shape: namely, the lining through one half of it. This is stretched at a distance of about six inches from the outer canvass; and, when closed at both ends, it forms a distinct inner room. The protection it affords against cold, or heat, may be put down at six degrees Fahrenheit. Thus, though my tent is so much less tall than a bell-tent, that its weight, together with that of the lining, little exceeds that of the other, yet the advantage in point of temperature is altogether on the side of the former; and in a land where extremes of heat and cold succeed each other rapidly, this is but another mode of saying, that the advantage in point of healthfulness is so likewise.

D

My servant's domicile, called in England a "patrol-tent," and a "kennel" here, stands close by, so as to be within hail, and is about six feet long, by three high. Two of the General's Aides have nothing better!

My furniture may be very shortly described: — A stretcher, or bedstead, formed of two wooden 6½ feet poles (each of which takes to pieces), connected by a strip of canvass 3 feet wide ; the latter being stretched tight by means of three pair of low, detachable, scissor-shaped legs, on the principle of a common camp-stool ;—one inch-thick mattrass and pillow ;— two waterproof blankets, or " water-decks;"—an iron wash-hand-stand which can be packed in a tin box ; the box serving as a tub, and its cover, when placed on the wash-hand-stand, forming a table (*Nota bene.* The common fault of such articles is, that they are made as high as if meant for use in England, whereas in a place where chairs are not, and where stretchers are the loftiest seats procurable, no table should stand more than a foot and three-quarters from the ground) ;—a very primitive Maltese canteen, consisting of a pan large enough to hold a kettle (which also serves,

or rather served, as teapot), a gridiron, three
tin cups without handles, three tin plates, two
knives and forks, two large and two small pew-
ter spoons (*Nota bene* again. The canteen-kettle
is generally made very shallow and broad,
to facilitate, I suppose, its stowage. But the
result is, that unless it is placed very evenly
on the fire, the highest portion of the bottom
is left dry, and becomes unsoldered. My own
is already rendered useless from this cause, and
I am consequently dependent on the General's);
—lastly, one portmanteau for my wardrobe,
and another in which are stowed some hermetically-sealed provisions, a case of Lemann's
biscuits, and a few soda-water bottles filled with
brandy and whiskey. Nothing hides the hard
brown earth; inasmuch as the tent and bedstead
bags, which might have been applied to the purpose, are a great deal more necessary for John,
who sleeps in the "kennel" on the ground.

It will convey to you some idea of the ad-
mirable order in camp, when I add, that
one of my boxes, containing things for which
I have no immediate use, is kept outside my
tent. Though the wood, at any rate, of which
it is composed, would be useful to many a sol-

dier who has to trudge to a distance for fuel, everybody assures me that it is perfectly safe. Indeed pilfering, so far as I can ascertain, is unheard of. Of what other community could the same be said ?

I don't suppose the foregoing enumeration of my possessions in the Crimea is so inviting as to put you out of conceit of your establishment in the Temple ; nevertheless, there are items in it, for which no equivalents, or substitutes, however paltry, are to be found among the majority of the Officers in camp. Thus in most tents, the means of ensuring personal cleanliness are absolutely wanting. The sea is too distant for bathing ; and though there are little springs in various neighbouring hollows, nobody has vessels which can be applied to washing. The men have only the small pans which they use in cooking; the Officers, destitute even of these, borrow them from the men, and manage, perhaps, such a toilet as can be accomplished with half a pint of water, unaided by towel, soap, nail-brush, tooth-brush, hair-brush, or comb ! Razors, naturally, are out of the question. Even before the landing, almost every one had abandoned them—from the bearded

Grenadier, whose face looks like a continuation of his own bearskin, to the callow Ensign, whose

"beauty draws us by a single hair."

Of course, it was the necessity, when they disembarked here, of bearing all their possessions on their backs, that reduced the Army to their worst trials. The sufferings entailed by actual fighting, by night-work in the trenches, or by a bivouac such as the troops were only relieved from five or six days ago, are bad enough; yet they are only part of the prospect contemplated by every man of sense when he adopts the military profession. But the unmentionable horrors of a state of things where neither the clothing can be changed, nor the body cleansed, for weeks on weeks!—when men born and trained as our Officers are born and trained, are found undergoing these, without a complaint on their lips — England may well be proud of her " gentlemen."

The Generals, Field-officers, and Staff, are somewhat better off; they possess basins and tubs; those who like it, can shave; and I have even seen a few white shirts, though they were not starched. Still, it was only the other day that even this portion of the Army got tents over their heads; and that you may not have too ex- alted a notion of their comforts, I will describe to you the costume in which I lately saw the Colonel of a regiment making his morning's report to General Brown. Both stood outside Sir George's tent, and I was one of a fumigating group not far off. The Colonel's black trou- sers hung in folds over his spurs, for lack of braces. His red coatee was fastened with three buttons, and showed to advantage a chocolate-coloured flannel shirt. The long ends of a silk neckcloth, tied in a sailor's knot, dangled over the coatee; and over all, was a dilapidated great coat, which had certainly not been brushed for the occasion. One hand he kept in his pocket; the other held a well- browned meerschaum; and with many vigo- rous pulls thereat, he told his story.

But to return. The day in camp begins, for me, when I hear the troops coming back to their tents after morning parade. Persons who have not tried it, might sup- pose, that the pounding from the fort-guns would act as an earlier *reveillée*. But to this the ear becomes habituated almost immediately. I have heard a General of Division say, that, while he sleeps easily enough through almost any amount of cannonading, the faintest report of a musket rouses him at once; for *that* indicates the approach of the enemy. As regards myself, not having to get up at either, I can sleep through both.

Directly after sunrise, the soldiers light their fires, and the Officers light their cigars, and chat over the night's work in cosy little groups, till the sun puts some warmth into them after the cold parade. Two or three of them were thus engaged yesterday before my tent, when I received the nearest introduction I have yet obtained to a Russian projectile. You must know, the sound made by the rushing of shot and shell through the air, is generally audible here; though we are so far from the fort guns that they cannot carry anything like the distance, unless fired at a great elevation. When this is the case, accuracy of aim is out of the question; and even if a ball does pay you a visit, it descends from such a height that it lies where it falls, and does no further mischief. A shell, however, is a more ugly

D 4

customer; and one, happening to alight, three
or four days ago, among the tents of the Fourth
Division, killed one man and wounded another.
The piece that did the mischief, is supposed to
be on board a certain man-of-war called the
"Twelve Apostles," which lies at the nearest,
or Southern extremity of the harbour.   She is
careened over before firing, in order to give
the mortar the highest possible elevation.

However, I have given you a very long
preface to a very simple, affair.   Our visitor
announced his approach in this wise:—First,
came the report of the discharge; then, a loud
noise, between a whistle and a whiz (a sort of
crescendo wheu-u-u-gh!), apparently quite close;
then, a *thud* against the ground, some thirty
yards past me; and then—a sense of the extreme
ease with which I had earned the respectability of
having been "under fire!"   The missile fell near
a donkey, without penetrating the hard ground
more than an inch or two; and, for a few
seconds, the soldiers round about, taking it
for a shell, gave it a wide berth, expecting to
see the poor jackass blown into fragments.
The spectacle not coming off, however, as soon
as was expected, some one went up, and dis-

covered the cause of all the excitement to be a plain unexplosive 32-pounder.

The donkey and myself, all this while, had kept our legs, though wiser animals threw themselves on their faces. In fact, the chief start my nerves sustained on the occasion, was from seeing one or two of my friends fall flat at my feet. This, however, I afterwards learnt, is quite the correct mark of respect to pay a passing shell, nor have I the slightest intention of omitting it for the future.

After the *matinée fumante*, comes breakfast; and then—equally a matter of course—a walk to the Picket-house. No account of Crimean camp-life would be complete without mention of this much-frequented lounge. It is a little ruin, appropriated, as its name imports, to one of the pickets, and is situated on the brow of the hill, two or three hundred yards in front of the Light Division. Thence it commands a view of Sebastopol to the left, and of the sea and the fleets to the right. There is a court-yard round it, with a wall about four feet high, behind which may perpetually be seen Officers with double eye-glasses, and telescopes, directed towards the town.

Sebastopol, seen from this point, appears
to be a handsome city, containing many
substantial public works, constructed out of
the light stone of the country. There are
no walls; so the talk about "breaching"
is — talk. But the place is defended on the
South side by a Round Tower, a Redan,
and various earthworks. The masts of the
"Twelve Apostles" are easily distinguishable.

Everything is preparing for the bombardment. The trenches were commenced the day
before yesterday, and a few guns, I believe, are
placed in position. They will remain silent, however, for the present, and until they can open
their fire to some purpose; as, of course, there
is no use in letting the enemy know beforehand
their true position and forwardness. Up to
this moment, though it is clear, from the increased activity of the fort batteries, that something is suspected, no shot or shell have
come near the working parties. Meanwhile,
waggons after waggons arrive from Balaklava,
filled with the fruits of the immense efforts
made at Varna to prepare munitions for the
siege. So incessant, I am told, was the labour
there imposed upon the troops, that a private

was heard to exclaim, that he supposed people at head-quarters now read the 4th commandment as, " Six days thou shalt make gabions and fascines, and the seventh day thou shalt have heavy-marching-order parade ! "

It does not appear whether the Russians have recovered from the fright they got on the 20th. A Polish deserter, who was taken the other day, said, that Menschikoff had given out, that our triumph at the Alma was entirely due to our superiority in fire-arms ; and that we could only be effectually opposed with the bayonet! The story, ridiculous as it sounds, receives some colour of probability from what one of our sentries has just seen. He got close enough to Sebastopol to observe a body of infantry practising charging at wooden boards — practising, moreover, *cheering* as they did so !

After spending the morning at the Picket-house, those who have nothing better to do, generally go, during the heat of the day, to their tents to read the newspapers. Of these we get a good supply, and, though they seem engrossed with what is doing here, they often bring news. Much is said about the harm they do by conveying information to the enemy. When, however, one considers the enormous quantity of rumours in camp that are affirmed one day, and contradicted the next—and the very few persons who can possibly know what is really doing, and being projected—it is difficult not to believe that the estimate of the evil is exaggerated. The Czar, one would rather suspect, must be situated in the matter much as is the poor Sultan with regard to his Bulgarian subjects, according to the Cadi in *Household Words*:—" Our father, the Sultan, knows how to deal with the Turks, for they always speak truth; and with the Greeks, for they always tell lies; but with the Bulgarians, who speak sometimes truth, and sometimes lies—with them, he knows not how to deal!"

The afternoon is always cool, and it is the best time for seeing the country, and for exploring among the curiosities of the camp. So the day passes till dinner. You are aware, I dare say, that there are no regimental messes here; but that the Officers generally club together in twos and threes. On my way home of an evening, my efforts are directed to breaking up some one or other of these parties, by carrying off a stray friend to share my scrambling repast; when John's inventive faculties are taxed to the utmost. Happily, my guests are easy to please; but I have already made the discovery, that my month's store of food is not quite so luxurious as it promised to be. The cans of hermetically-sealed cooked meats which I brought out, labelled "Lamb and Peas," "Boiled Beef," "Haricot Mutton," and bearing a dozen other equally imposing titles, are certainly better than nothing — but that is all I can say of them. The meat is cooked to rags, and these, again, are lubricated by masses of fat. No invalid could touch them. Why gelatine should not be resorted to, instead of grease (as in the case of Hogarth's Essence of Beef, and of the preserved soups), I don't know.

If I were to lay in a fresh commissariat (you may tell your military friends), I would bring lemons, to counteract these adipose preparations, and to supply, in a sanitary point of view, the place of vegetables. I would also try to get the French caked preparation of vegetables themselves; and I would certainly put up some tins of the English patented paste of preserved milk and chocolate — the preserved milk *alone* is not worth its room.

This, however, is a digression. Practically, and so long as a man is well, his camp-appetite is equal to most things. The dinner equipage may be scanty; but, by dint of a bold nomenclature, its shortcomings are gracefully veiled. Thus, one talks of a "glass" of wine, though that liquor (supposing you to possess it) is served in a handleless tin mug — the same mug which, in the course of the evening, will figure as a "cup" or a "tumbler," according as it may be charged with coffee, or whiskey-toddy. Smoke, moreover, with which the repast invariably concludes, covers a multitude of sins in the preceding arrangements — but not smoke of Turkish chibouques, nor of mild, romantic, Oriental tobacco. Cavendish and shag — short clays and meerschaums — and cigars, when they can be got — maintain their ground in the taste of the campaigners, despite of their Eastern experience; and a ship-load of such supplies, would, no doubt, be easily sold here.

Everybody turns in by half-past nine. By ten, the last fires have gone out, the last araba has

screeched past with its load ; and—but for the
long spectral crowd of tents that you see glimmering through the distance, as you lace up
your doors for the night—you might believe
yourself in the wilderness.

Such is a general description of a day in
camp; but yesterday, being Sunday, the rou-
tine was broken by the impressive ceremony of
an open-air Church-parade. Each Division, on
these occasions, has divine service performed
by its own Chaplain. Ours was drawn up on
the rising ground, just beyond the tents, in
a dense hollow square. The Clergyman and
Officers occupied the centre. Every one was
covered. Some of the men wore forage-
caps, for lack of shakos ; and *on dit* that the
loss of these stiff and ugly varieties of head-
gear is submitted to with great resignation by
the Line generally. The Chaplain, with his
dark velvet skull-cap, and black moustache
and beard, reminded me of a foreign padre in
canonicals.

We were scarcely placed in position, before
the loud rush of round-shot from the fort was
heard, again and again, in our ears, causing
sundry dislocations of the square — the men

grinning and swaying about at each whirr
in a kind of jocular disorder. Nothing was
left for it but to move off. So we took up our
ground a few hundred yards lower down; and
here — though a fleecy little cloudlet, which
announced its birth in a thunder-clap, showed
that a shell had burst above us, not very far
off to our rear—the service was conducted to
a close. Every body, of course, stands, upon
these occasions, throughout the ceremony. To
obviate fatigue, therefore, the Litany and Com-
munion are omitted. The Chaplain preached
extemporaneously, and with so excellent a
voice, that, though the wind was blowing his
surplice about, it did not drown his tones. I was
amused by his British *sang froid*. Half his con-
gregation might perish round the walls of Sebastopol before next Church-parade—a theme
which the threatening missiles exploding about
him, would have served sufficiently well to en-
force—but he utterly disdained such obvious
rhetoric. Perhaps, indeed, it is considered
undesirable to allude to subjects of the kind;
and certainly they are too patent to need much
insisting on. At any rate, the reverend
gentleman neither noticed the pyrotechnics

in his sound practical sermon, nor in his own person; but stood with his back to the fort, and preached on some everyday text, and never changed his voice, or turned his head, in compliment to shot or shell.

Next day the Division moved its quarters two or three hundred yards further from the enemy.

LETTER V.

I DARE say you think it is time that I should fulfil my promise of giving you a general description of the camp; but I confess, I do not even now approach so large a subject without trepidation. No one but a military man can treat it properly. However, if you will take the following "notions" for what they are worth — as the impressions of a *pékin*, who pretends not to professional accuracy — why, perhaps, they may help you in any after inquiries into the subject, or, possibly, throw light on some of the more authoritative accounts that will reach you from hence.

Nothing can be imagined more dreary and barren than the country in which the camp is pitched. Though, in reality, an elevated table land, it is so extensive that it produces the effect of an undulating plain. The high distant hills beyond its Eastern and Southern extremities, are thus comparatively dwarfed. The sea is hidden by rising ground to the

Westward. The highest side of the plateau is towards the North, and the camp is placed two or three hundred yards below the summit. This summit is crossed by several gorges; and from it, there is a slope Northward, about a mile and a half long, down to Sebastopol.

The colouring of the scenery is simple enough — namely, plain drab. No vegetation is visible. There are, indeed, good vineyards (now sear, and stripped of grapes) in the hollows near Balaklava; and there are cultivated strips at the sheltered bottoms of most of the gorges where water is found; but such oases lie too low to affect the general landscape. Elsewhere, the grass is scanty and withered: There are no trees, only here and there patches of short oak scrub. Even the withered grass and the scrub must be looked for. As a rule, one sees nothing but bare brown earth, strewn with rough stones that set their faces against galloping Aide-de-camps; or bristling with bunches of burnt-up, star-headed, thistles, of which the best that can be said, is, that they now and then shelter a misguided anemone.

Flecking this tawny Sahara, in a line from

East to West, is the British camp. It is three or four miles long, and reaches from the Eastern extremity of the plateau to a ravine on our left; whence the French lines continue the *cordon* to the sea. Picture to yourself a triple line of those bell-shaped red-tipped tents which you remember at Chobham. In front, and within a few feet of them, stand all the firelocks, in a single row of tripods—each bayonet being surmounted by the shako of its owner. One can thus tell the Guards' camp from the row of bearskins, the lines of the Highlanders from the plumes, and so forth; though the heroes themselves may be cooking their dinners, or otherwise non-apparent. Moreover, this arrangement, in case of an alarm, enables the men to find their arms at once, and in the very places on which the regiments would naturally stand when forming line.

Every tent (I assume you to be looking towards the front) is pitched about eight yards off its side-neighbour, and (in order to give room for the cooking-fires) about twice that distance from the one before, or behind, it. To the rear of the whole triple row — but laterally more distant from each other — are the tents of the Generals, the Field Officers, and the Staff. Behind these, again, are hospital-marquees, picquetted horses, bullock-waggons, &c. &c.

My description, however — if you have had the patience to follow it — will give you much too formal an idea of the effect of the lines, unless you allow for the curves produced by inequalities of ground, and for the long intervals between separate Divisions. The truth is, that except at particular spots, where the symmetry of certain portions becomes apparent, the camp seems to consist of long straggling crowds of tents, variously distributed, though following a certain general direction. There are, moreover, only two or three heights whence a view of the whole line can be obtained.

The Army is divided into six Divisions. They are thus placed : — The Second Division occupies the extreme right; behind it, in reserve, is the First; to the left of the Second, is the Light Division; after which, following the same direction, comes the Fourth; the Third holds the extreme left; and the Cavalry Division is at Balaklava. As a knowledge

of the composition of these Divisions is necessary for comprehending even the public de-
spatches, and as you cannot obtain it from the
Army List, you may probably find the sub-
joined memorandum useful:—

The Light Division consists of the 7th, 19th,
23rd, 33rd, 77th, and 88th regiments; with
the 2nd battalion of the Rifle Brigade :

The First Division consists of the Grenadier,
Coldstream, and Scots Fusileers, Guards; and
of the 42nd, 79th, and 93rd, Highlanders:

The Second Division consists of the 30th,
41st, 47th, 49th, 55th, and 95th regiments :

The Third Division consists of the 1st, 4th,
28th, 38th, 44th, and 50th regiments :

The Fourth Division consists of the 20th,
21st, 46th, 57th, 63rd, and 65th regiments;
with the 1st battalion of the Rifle Brigade :

The Cavalry Division consists of the 4th and
5th Dragoon Guards, the 1st, 2nd, 4th, 6th, 8th,
13th and 17th Dragoons, and the 11th Hussars.

To these must be added the 1500 Sailors,
who are encamped between the Fourth and
Light Divisions; a detachment of Sappers
and Miners; the troops of Horse Artillery
attached to each Division, and the Marines

at Balaklava.   A Chaplain of the Church of
England, and, I believe, a Roman Catholic
Priest, attends every Division.   There are no
women, native or imported.

The regimental tents form, as I have mentioned, a line which is only three deep.   According to camp rules, the tents of each company are arranged in a row running from front
to rear; the men occupying the front, and the
Officers the rear.   The only tents behind these
are those appropriated to the Staff, Field Officers, &c.   Thus the depth of the general line
depends upon the number of tents allowed to
the men and Officers of a single company.
Here, the allowance is two to the men, and one
to the Officers ; but so diminished is the effective force of each regiment, that there are not,
I believe, on an average, more than sixteen men,
or four Officers, to each tent.   Of course, many
inconveniences must attend a total absence of
privacy; but, these apart, I should think that,
in a place where people need little or no room
for stowing away their possessions, and where
the nights are often bitterly cold, close pack-
ing can be no very great hardship.

All the tents have little trenches, about a foot

wide, and four or five inches deep, dug round
them to carry off water, in case of rain. Cooking, of course, goes on outside. The men make
little fireplaces with a couple of stones, crossed
with two or three bars made out of the hoops
of ration-casks; and the whole is protected by
a semicircle of some half dozen more stones
against the wind. Fuel is obtained from the
patches of outlying brushwood, which are in
danger of being soon exhausted. Each man
has his pot for boiling, and cooks his own
food. The rations allowed *per diem* are,
I believe, 1½lb. of biscuit, 1lb. of salt meat,
and half a gill of rum. Coffee is also served
out; but I have not taken pains to ascertain
the exact quantity, seeing that it is given
the men, not only unground, but raw, and
they have nothing either to roast, or grind it
with. *Au reste*, the rations are excellent of
their kind, and are, I believe, varied with
fresh meat twice a-week.

Good drinking water is obtained from the
springs at the bottoms of the neighbouring
ravines. It is brought to camp in blue wooden
kegs, called canteens.

No oats, I hear, can be got for the horses.

This is a great misfortune; for though the country nags thrive well enough on hay and barley, such a diet is found to "blow out" our English steeds.

Tobacco the men have to buy for themselves. It is, moreover, difficult to procure, as you may judge from the following anecdote. Two privates had got hold of a goose, which they intended for their own consumption. An Officer coveting the bird, offered 10s. for it, and was refused. A few minutes afterwards, the men bartered it with somebody else for a lump of tobacco which, in England, might have cost twopence! To people at home, this deficiency of the "fragrant weed" may appear a very slight evil, if not an actual advantage. The fact is, however, that in camp, tobacco is almost a necessary of life. Smoking is decidedly a good stop-gap and palliative; and, in proportion to a man's actual wants and hardships, he is driven to resort to it. I think it is Dickens who introduces a character, to whom it is said to have been "bed, board, lodging, and washing." That is precisely what it is out here to nearly everybody. When the Army go back to veritable beds, wholesome living, warm houses, and soap, it will be time enough to rail against their pipes. Meanwhile, I should like to see the wholesale denouncer either of tobacco or fermented liquors, sent to digest his own arguments, without the one or the other, for twenty-four hours in the trenches. Recollect, our men go out to the works at 4 A. M., and are not themselves relieved till the same hour next day. What is it to these poor fellows, lying on their stomachs to avoid shot and shell, all through the bitter night, on the bare ground, that total abstinence promotes longevity? The question with them, is how to keep alive till they are relieved next morning; and, without a little rum and tobacco, they would often find it difficult to do so.

As regards the provision for the sick and wounded, there is a double-poled hospital marquee attached to each Brigade; and ambulance-carts are used for conveying such patients as require more care and comforts than can be afforded them in camp, to Balaklava. At that place, there are, I believe, two hospitals; and, if these happen to be full, there are transports always plying to Scutari. The wounded are carried on what are called stretchers — long narrow wooden frames, stretched over with canvass, and with the poles extending at both ends, so as to admit of being borne by two men. The members of the regimental Bands, whose musical functions are in abeyance during the campaign, are employed in this office.

I believe that everything, within the scope of ordinary foresight, has been done by the home authorities to render the Medical Department effective. Still there are many facts which show the necessity of further measures. You are aware, of course, that a large proportion of the Surgeons sent out with the expedition had to return home sick, before the landing in the Crimea. As regards the Medical Officers who remain in the field, there is unhappily so much cholera (though it is diminishing), diarrhœa, dysentery, and fever, that they are fully employed from morning to night. What will they do, when some bloody engagement triples, and quadruples, their work? On the other hand, there is a palpable difficulty about permanently increasing the Medical Staff of the Army to a numerical strength which is only called for by a temporary emergency; while if an extra number are to be engaged *pro hâc vice* merely, they must, of course, be paid much higher allowances than are received by their colleagues *en permanence*.

As a palliative measure — or, perhaps, in any case — it might be advisable to retain the services of a lower grade of men. I heard a story, the other day, about a soldier, who, after some bloody affair, lay in the trenches, apparently in the last stage of cholera. A couple of men passed by with a stretcher, exclaiming that there was clearly no use in picking *him* up. "Don't you be in a *'urry*," gasped the poor soul, "I'm not dead *yet!*—I daresay I should do well enough, if I could only get something *'ot!*" So strenuous an appeal was irresistible, and they carried him off. But I hope his recovery did not depend on the speedy administration of the treatment he himself indicated; for, pending the demand at that moment for the scalpel and the saw, "something *'ot*" was the last thing he was likely to get. Now, there are few men, however slight their knowledge of medicine, who could not be of use in such cases as this. They might apply friction; put on hot flannels, and mustard poultices; they might, in short, administer a hundred simple remedies which would save valuable lives; and that, with no better skill than they could pick up from the general instructions which, of course, would be issued to them by the regular Medical Staff. More than one Officer has told me with his own lips, that he ascribed his recovery from cholera to the untiring efforts of some friend, who rubbed and rubbed away, for hours, at the bloodless skin, till circulation was restored. But who is to apply such protracted remedies to the common soldier? It can only be done by retaining a far greater number of hospital assistants. And adequate funds, I suppose, will not be forthcoming for such a purpose, unless we resort to the comparatively low-paid class of unskilled labour.

Pillows, for the wounded, are sadly wanted both here and at Scutari.

With respect to the Medical Stores, they were sent from England in abundance to Malta; but the case I lately mentioned to you of the transport "Cambria," would make it appear, that they have not been sufficiently drawn upon. Rice is a great remedy in the various bowel complaints that prevail, and I have not heard that it is deficient; but there are other articles of diet for invalids, the necessity of which was not so easily suggested by the experience of Medical Officers in England. For instance; at home, a compound of opium and calomel is, I believe, very commonly exhibited in cases of diarrhœa. Now, out here, the administration of such medicine, in any thing like the proportions in which it is given to patients living in houses, would be impossible. A tent in the Crimea, with steppe-winds blowing, is too cold, in any case, for much calomel; but for a man afflicted with a disease which is constantly depriving him even of the indifferent shelter which that tent affords, such treatment would be fatal. Port-wine is found to be of great service under these circumstances. There is, however, far too little of it to admit of its being freely administered.

With regard to vegetables, they cannot, of course, be sent out here in their natural state; but there is a French patent, under which they are pressed by steam power into thin cakes, which remain fresh for any length of time. Why not procure supplies of these? A square inch expands, after boiling, into ten times its size, and supplies enough for a meal. I have myself some Brussels-sprouts, prepared under this patent, which were given me by an Officer, and I often use them, and find them tolerable, though a little more bitter than the unsophisticated originals. The desideratum is, however, to supply, not a dainty, but a powerful sanitary agent.

Once more; if our sailors, even in health, are supplied with lemon juice, why should the soldiers be without it?

There is no denying, that the troops suffer greatly from disease. The extent to which they do so, may be conjectured from the fact, that in the four weeks after the Army landed in the Crimea, its effective strength* had been

---

* Left Varna :—

> 23,500 infantry,
> 2,000 artillery,
> 1,000 cavalry,
> 600 sappers and miners.

Total force 27,100

reduced by 7000. Placing (in round numbers) 2000 of this amount to the account of the Battle of the Alma, there remains 5000 to be put down to disease. Cholera has, happily, almost ceased; but hardly any body escapes from some form or other of bowel-complaint. So great is the liability to diarrhœa, that very slight doses of ordinary cathartics are sufficient to bring it on. The bleak winds, which come and go here so suddenly, have the peculiarity of invariably aggravating its amount. Cold in England attacks you manfully in the head, throat, or chest: here it always hits you under the waistcoat. Many Officers wear, as a preservative, red woollen sashes, tied several times round the hips; in fact, the *kumur-bund* of Eastern nations, who, I suppose, did not adopt it without some such good cause. A blue or green sash is part of the uniform of the *Zouaves*, and of the *Indigènes;* but the French Officers, like our own, affect the red ones, as being, I presume, more picturesque.

Apropos of the French, let me wind up this long account with some noticeable points of difference between their camp-ways and ours.

If it is lawful to learn from an enemy, one may certainly take hints from an ally. I do not pretend to decide the merits of the tent controversy. You know, of course, that every French soldier carries his own little piece of a tent on his back; that three or more of these can be fastened together; and that thus they escape the risk of ever having to bivouac, as our poor fellows did on their first arrival here. On the one hand, it is said, that the weight the Frenchman has to carry, is thus greatly increased, so as to interfere with his power of making rapid forced marches; while the tents themselves do not afford one quarter as much comfort and space as a bell-tent. On the other hand, one must admit, that it is in those very campaigns which involve the greatest number of forced marches, that the means of conveying our bell-tents would oftenest be found wanting. But whatever may be the true deduction to make from these *pros* and *cons*, as regards campaigns in general, there can be no doubt, that, on an expedition like the present one, with nothing about it of a roving character, the British soldier is the best housed.

F

As regards diet, the following differences are the most striking.

The French soldiers have flour served out to them, instead of biscuit, and bake their own bread. General Canrobert handsomely distributed one day's supply lately to every soldier in the British camp.

In the next place, one Frenchman cooks for twelve, instead of each man, as with us, preparing his own dinner. They carry out, in other words, the old principle of the Division of Labour. The office is taken by rotation. Amongst other advantages arising from this arrangement, a few large *marmites* serve for a whole regiment, instead of every man being cumbered with his particular pots and pans. But above all, by its means, a more palatable and wholesome dinner for the troops is secured. So it might be with us. For instance, nothing can be better than our ration-pork when it has been well soaked for two or three hours before being dressed; nor anything more salt, and hence more likely to aggravate the diseases prevalent in camp, than the same pork, when cooked without the initiatory process in question. It is, of course,

impossible for each of our soldiers, amidst the
various calls on him, to spare every day the
time necessary for soaking his pork; but one
man in twelve might, I suppose, very easily
do so.

Again: the French soldier carries, by way of
water-flask, a light flat tin vessel, like a shallow
canister, about six inches long by two deep;
slightly curved longitudinally, to suit the shape
of his body; and slung across his shoulders by a
strap. There are two orifices in the top: one is
stopped by a cork, and is surmounted by a short
fixed funnel; to admit of being conveniently
placed to the lips for drinking, or of passing
liquid into the flask without waste. The other
orifice has a conical pipe, about an inch long, attached to it, so small at the top, that water cannot easily be spilt from it, and at the same time,
large enough to admit of the soldier sucking a
mouthful through it, if he is thirsty. This
flask, or *bidon*, as it is called, costs in France
about a franc. It is covered with cloth by the
men themselves, to keep the tin from soiling
their uniforms.

In remarkable contrast with it, is the
blue keg, or canteen, with which the En-

glishman is afflicted. First, it is made of
wood, and carries therefore less liquid, in proportion to its size, and is less easily rinsed out,
than if it were made of tin. Secondly, it is
about twice as deep as a *bidon,* has no-curve
to fit the body, is (I should guess) half-a-dozen
times as heavy, and, being round, like a tub cut
short, takes up more space laterally. Thirdly,
its orifice, being neither more nor less than a
bung-hole, is not well adapted for receiving
and conducting liquid into the canteen without
the aid of a funnel, and is, of course, particularly
awkward to drink from. Lastly, it must cost
twice the sum. There is, in fact, but this
to be said for it — it dates from the days of
Marlborough !

One other point of difference between the two
camp systems remains to be stated. The members of our Bands are, as I have said, devoted
to bearing stretchers. The French musicians,
on the contrary, are, at this moment, playing
" Rule Britannia," in compliment to the *entente
cordiale;* and many a poor sick Briton is, I
dare say, raising himself on his elbow, to catch
the faint, but cheering strains, as they float
to our lines. Our Allies argue, that camp is

the very place where music is wanted; that a soldier can carry a stretcher into action as well as an accomplished musician, but that, if both get knocked on the head, a month's training will replace the one, and not the other. They add, that even if the musician alone will serve our turn, it would be well that he should, at any rate, play during the days and weeks that happily intervene between bloody engagements, in the most active warfare. Can you answer this Gallic view of the case ?

LETTER VI.

SINCE my letter of the 9th, everything here has received a great impulse. Dissatisfied, I suppose, with the information brought by their cowardly Cossacks, who invariably scamper off at the first shot of our pickets — the Russians made, on the afternoon of that day, a grand reconnoissance on our right front. It occurred about three o'clock, too late for me to tell you about it by that opportunity. I had noticed an unusual scuffling of feet, when John ran in to my tent, to apprise me that the enemy were in sight of the camp. I went out, and there, true enough, were the Russians on the crest of the hill, with a few mounted Officers in advance of them. Our troops were already in line; horse artillery were scudding to the right, and everything seemed to promise a general action on our own ground.

Under these circumstances, I made my dispositions both for seeing the sport, and for beating a retreat if necessary. Putting my money, some biscuits, and a flask of brandy into my own pocket, I told John to put half a dozen " concentrated beefs" into his; to wait where he was, till I came back, and to lie on his face, if the round shot and canister grew unpleasant. He behaved perfectly well, and promised obedience. I then borrowed —— 's pony, and sticking a revolver (don't laugh!) into my holster, rode up and down behind the whole length of the lines to see the arrangements. The troops merely stood before the tents, with the Generals and Staff in front; waiting, I suppose, for the Russians to make the first move. This, however, the latter had no intention of doing; and, after exposing everybody to an hour or two of bitter bleak wind, they retired. I confess I was gratified, on coming back half frozen, to find my new domestic and traps where I left them. But it is only fair to add, that, so far as I could see, the camp-servants, generally, behaved quite as quietly as if the enemy had been all the while in Sebastopol.

Sir Edmund Lyons happened to have ridden here from head-quarters (where he goes pretty nearly every day) just in time to see the turn-out.

I don't know whether this affair gave the Russians a better notion of the position of our works than they previously possessed, but on the 11th, they contrived to kill two men, and wound two more, at the trenches. Soon afterwards, Lord Raglan decided on employing sharpshooters to approach the enemy's batteries, and to pick off the gunners at the embrasures; and the men were invited to volunteer for the purpose. Nothing can better indicate how little the *morale* of the poor fellows is broken by all the hardships they are undergoing, than the fact that, though only six out of each corps were required for this dangerous work, no less than twenty-six men out of a single regiment offered their services. The duty, however, was one requiring skill quite as much as courage; so, in the end, I believe, the best marksmen were taken, irrespectively of their own inclinations in the matter.

The bombardment of the town was, about the same time, announced to take place on the 17th. The Ships were to join; and many persons expected that it would be a matter of a few hours, followed by an assault.

Such being the state of affairs, about nine

o'clock on the previous night, I could not
help walking through various portions of the
camp, to see what effect was produced by the
prospect of so deadly a conflict on the men
about to be engaged in it. The soldiers,
worn out with toil and disease, were perfectly
silent, and were preparing to go to sleep, precisely as usual. The sailors, on the contrary,
who had been hard at work, ever since their
arrival, in hauling huge ship-guns up the
heights, had got lights in their tents, and were
indulging in every species of fun and lark.
There was one tent in particular which I
noticed, in which a jolly tar, gifted with a
piercing falsetto, was aping a woman, and
singing a song in the highest possible treble,
and with such comical airs and graces, that
the place rang with roars of merriment, and
approving bravos, from his comrades. But it
was a touching contrast. Something, no doubt,
was due to Jack's proverbial light-hearted-
ness; but much also to the fact, that he was
comparatively fresh from his ships, and was
in the *condition* natural to Englishmen. Not
so, the poor soldiers, who have been running
the gauntlet of exposure and disease, month

after month, until, as an Officer lately observed to me, they can hardly be recognised
as the same men who landed at Gallipoli.
Some such reflections, I suppose, prompted
the following lines, which were written by a
man who lives not far from my tent :—

" THE EVE OF THE BOMBARDMENT.

O'er against the leaguered city, countless tents are gleaming
    white—
Silent, save where, crowding gaily, England's sailors rouse the
    night
        With jest and laugh and chorus'd song,
        By flick'ring camp-fires stretched along.

On our muskets sadly leaning, list we to our comrades' mirth,
As each hearty shout reminds us of the Land that gave us birth:
        So—ere a felon clime could smite
        Us down—so leapt *our* pulses light!

Ah! 'tis long since Cheer and Revel from our pest-worn lines
    have shrunk:
Yet a thought of comfort stirs us, musing on the thousands sunk
        Beneath a foe that mocks our ken—
        To-morrow we shall fight with *men!*

Welcome steel—the onset welcome, fiery shell and glancing
    glaive—
So we perish not like lepers—so we 'scape the lazar-grave,
        Heaped up in hurried stealth and gloom,
        Without a stone to mark our doom!

Hastes the Hour for which we've laboured, nightly 'neath our
  starry pall,
Digging close the circling trenches, piling firm the gabion-wall,
    While ever on the thund'ring town
    Our sheeted Camp looked stilly down.

Not an answering shot has sounded; hoarded vengeance waits—
  'till morn!
So the serpent's prey, imprisoned, strikes with frantic hoof and
  horn,
    While, coiled in many a giant ring,
    He nor speeds, nor stays, his spring.

Foes! whom, hating not, we hold as victims to a despot's pride!
Nobler victims to his madness, conquering, crimsoned Alma's
  tide—
    Along the gory path they trod,
    Bear *ye* the tyrant's name to God!"

It was arranged that the bombardment was
to begin at half-past six on the morning of the
17th, upon two shells being fired by the
French batteries. A quarter of an hour before
the time, I found myself in the court of the
Picket-house, among a little crowd of Generals
and Staff-Officers, who were all levelling their
glasses at the town, in anxious expectation of
the spectacle. But already the smoke of the
Russian batteries, aided by the wind, had so
enveloped the whole place, that little was to
be seen except the Round Tower, which stands
somewhat in advance of the other works, and

to the British right. Somehow or other, the
appointed signal was not made to time; so
the Seaman's Battery opened the ball. In a
few seconds, another battery followed, and
before half a minute, a long irregular line of
jets of smoke had made the position of the
British trenches no more a secret to any one.
Amidst the general din — which, however, was
not overpowering, as nobody had to raise his
voice in talking — the rush of the shot from
the Lancaster guns through the air was dis-
tinctly audible. Its resemblance to the pant-
ing-sound of a railway engine in motion became at once the subject of remark. As some
Paddy observed, " it was the noise of an ex-
press-train that stopped at no intermadiate
stations!" The Round Tower was apparently the principal object of the new projectile. Indeed, most of the batteries
seemed to have selected that unhappy edi-
fice for their mark. To the spectators in
the Picket-house, no arrangement could have
been more agreeable, as the smoke prevented
us from easily discerning any other target.
For some time the shots fell a little short, but
at length a 68-pounder from the Seaman's
Battery hit it full, and made a gap that could

be seen with the naked eye. The tower was soon scarred all over, but the men inside it stood pluckily to their guns, despite the heavy odds against them, for about an hour, when it was silenced; and the bombardment thenceforward became all smoke and noise.

During this time, I had been trying to sketch the scene — I need not send you the result, as you will obtain a sufficiently clear idea of it by referring back to *Punch's* picture of the Naval Review. But the sketch finished, and break-fast time having arrived, I returned to my tent, leaving behind, amongst other Officers, Sir George Brown. The General was soon afterwards joined by the Duke of Cambridge, who had also been there earlier in the morn-ing. While they were engaged in talking behind the low wall, a round shot came up from the fort, lighted on the wall just between them, and after making a playful bound or two between the building and the side of the court, fell spent against the back of it.

A second shot had been seen approaching when I was there, to which a general obeisance had been made; but it stopped short. I should add, that there are always a few balls lying in front of the place, though the enemy seldom manage to fire past it.

While I was in my tent, a grand explosion occurred, evidently that of a powder-cart or magazine. I was out in a moment, and saw a white column of smoke towering above the hill between us and the works, and surmounted by a head of tight little curls, which gradually opened out, till the whole resembled — if you will forgive so homely a figure — a gigantic cauliflower. The men cheered vociferously, and I believe I joined them; but we subsequently learnt, that it was one of our own ammunition-waggons that had given our lungs so much play.

The Ships did not contribute their quota to the entertainment till half-past one. The continuous muffled roar of their distant broadsides was very grand. Curiously enough, though it seemed far less loud than the cannonade from the trenches, it alone had the effect of making my tent-poles vibrate. The two sounds together reminded me (my head must have been full that day of household images) of a gusty corridor in an old mansion; the naval broadsides were the long rattling of distant window-frames, and the shots from the trenches the sharp banging of doors.

I again visited the Picket-house in the evening, and found that the French guns had ceased firing, in consequence of a powder-magazine exploding, so that the enemy were paying us their undivided attentions. The shells looked like revolving lights as it grew dark, and I was tempted to accompany a picket of the 19th Regiment, then going to guard the left Lancaster battery. This was my first visit to the trenches. The night covered us effectually on our way, and when there, the compact nine-feet-high wall of bank and gabions and sand-bags, against which the Officer in command and myself reclined, seemed a very fair security against round-shot to those who had nothing to do with the embrasures. Poor Captain Rowley was, indeed, killed by one that bounded down on him from the top of the parapet as he lay in the trench; but this must be a rare case. Shell, of course, are inconvenient in all situations of life, but at night they are less so than at other times, as one can see them coming, and scud out of the way. In fact, I had promised myself a very pleasant pyrotechnical evening in com-

pany with the Officer who had invited me
down; but the reports from the enemy's batteries gradually diminished in frequency; and
at length there came an order to the gentleman in charge of the gun to cease firing for
the night. So I retired, having not done much
more than ascertain, that the enemy's practice had been sufficiently good during the day
to prove, that the perpetual pounding away
that has been going on from the town for the
last fortnight, has, at any rate, taught them
the range of their metal.

That night, the Russians threw up earthworks which enfiladed the French guns, and
swept many of them out of their embrasures;
which, coupled with the explosion of two powder
magazines, kept our gallant Allies silent all
yesterday. The Besiegers employèd last night,
and the one before, in repairing the mischief
done to their works during the day — and
so did the Besieged! The croakers are tri-
umphant. I have got the prevalent malady (I
don't mean croaking); and though port wine
and Dr. —— are bringing me round, I am
half afraid I shall have to go on board ship
before the town is taken, after all.

LETTER VII.

THOUGH little has been done worth writing about since my last letter, I have lately ascertained some particulars respecting the share of the Fleets in the affair of the 17th, which will, I think, interest you. Of course, you will have heard before this arrives, that, except a good shaking given to Fort Constantine, where two embrasures were knocked into one—little damage was done to the enemy's works by the Allied navies on the occasion in question. I do not pretend to know what may have been the objects of the demonstration, or how far they were accomplished; but the moot question of Ships *versus* Forts certainly remains unaffected by it. This will be apparent from the account which I am going to give you, of the positions taken by the various English, French, and Turkish vessels.

No less an authority, on such matters, than the present Governor of Malta, has, I believe, laid it down, that 300 yards is the smallest dis-

G

tance at which a fort should be built from
the shore, that being the range within which
men-of-war can concentrate their broadsides,
so as to be a match for stone-walls. The shoals
round Sebastopol made it impossible for the
British ships to approach to anything like this
degree of nearness; and all, except two, lay
off at distances varying from 1000 to 1700
yards. The following was the order of battle. I cannot guarantee the absolute preci-
sion of the distances; but I think you may
rely on their *relative* accuracy.

Let us begin with the Britannia. Place a
good map of the coast before you, and describe a circle, having its centre at Cape Constantine, with a radius of 1720 yards, and
another circle having its centre at Cape Alexander, with a radius of 1990 yards; and the
Western point of intersection will give you the
position of Admiral Dundas's ship. Alter the
first radius to 770 yards, and the second to
1590, and the same process will give you
that of the Agamemnon. Substitute 1208
for 770, and 2280 for 1590, and the point
of contact will show the position of the Terrible. The British ships were arranged in a form

something like a pair of compasses, nearly closed, and *minus* half of one leg. Speaking more precisely, it was an acute angle, formed by two irregular lines, which, sloping towards the North-East from the Britannia and the Agamemnon, met at the Terrible. I will now write their names in the order which they would take in the imaginary figure I have described:—

British Line.	Towed by	Distance in yards from Cape Constantine.
Britannia	Furious	1720
Trafalgar	Retribution	1620
Vengeance . . .	Highflyer	1580
Rodney	Spiteful	1300
Bellerophon . . .	Cyclops	1160
Queen	Vesuvius	1140
Lynx (look-out ship)	——	1140
Sphynx (ditto)	——	1150
Tribune (ditto)	——	1340
Sampson (ditto)	——	1340
Terrible (ditto)	—— . . , , .	1410

Then, returning in a direction back towards the South-West, the

Albion	Firebrand	1280
Arethusa	Triton	1140
London	Niger	1040
Sanspareil	——	880
Agamemnon . . .	——	770

The Spiteful occupied a place inside the

angle, between the London and the Sphinx. I have indicated all the ships by their distances from Cape Constantine, because it is necessary to have a common standard of comparisons; but you will, of course, remember, that the Agamemnon, and all the vessels north of her, were also exposed to the Telegraph and Wasp Forts, as well as to some recent earthworks, higher up the coast. Some of these ships were, indeed, much closer to the last-mentioned forts than to Fort Constantine.

The French and Turkish men-of-war took up their positions in a line stretching in a South-by-South-Westerly direction from the Britannia, to a point within 260 yards from the shore. They were placed in the following order:—

French and Turkish Line.	Towed by
Napoléon	——
Henri IV.	Canada.
Mahmoudie . . .	Turkish Admiral.
Valmy	Descartes.
Ville de Paris . .	Primoguet.
Jupiter	Christophero Colombo.
Turkish (two-decker)	——
Friedland	Vauban.
Marengo	Labrador.
Montebello . . .	——
Suffren	Albatros.
Jean Bart	——
Charlemagne . . .	——

I should add that these lists represent the order and composition of the lines at half-past one, when they opened fire; but, by half-past five, the following were almost the only ships engaged with the forts: — Agamemnon, Sanspareil, Rodney (on shore), Bellerophon, Queen, Sampson, Terrible, Spitfire, and Sphynx.

I have received another account, which puts the Britannia at 2500 yards, and the Agamemnon at 800 yards, from Fort Constantine; and which places the latter ship at 750 from the Telegraph Fort, and at 1200 from the Wasp Fort. As regards Fort Constantine, perhaps the apparent difference may be explained by the position of its batteries on the coast. The first scale is measured, not from the batteries, but from the Cape.

The sea round Sebastopol is so shallow, that even at the place occupied by the Britannia there are only fifteen fathoms water; while Admiral Lyons, who pushed his ship—no prophet was needed to predict it — as far as she could go (into five and a quarter fathoms), did not get closer than the point I have above indicated.

In spite of the distance, the Agamemnon and Sanspareil (a soldier gravely mentioned her to me the other day, as the *Sarsapareil*) shook Fort Constantine so terribly between them, that I suppose it will always be a question, how much the vast naval forces of the Allies might not have effected, had it been deemed expedient for them all to anchor as close along shore as their draught of water permitted. The experience of Sir Edmund Lyons and Captain Dacres seems to show, that the injury to the Fleets, in such a case, and in the *then* state of things, would not have been so great as might be imagined. The enemy, not contemplating so near an approach of our men-of-war, had constructed their embrasures in a mode that did not admit of the guns being easily depressed to the level of the hulls of ships only 800 yards distant. Thus, though the Agamemnon was hit no less than 217 times, nearly all the damage she sustained was in her rigging; and of the 650 persons on board, there were only four killed and twenty-six wounded. On the other hand, the Sanspareil, being compelled to retire for twenty-six minutes, suffered, proportionally, far more injury during her temporary retreat, than when she was in her original position.

It must be recollected, too, that the damage sustained in these two cases, was, of course, enhanced by the isolation of the vessels, and by the concentrated fire which the enemy was thus enabled to bring to bear on them. The Agamemnon was so hard pressed from this cause (during the short absence of the Sanspareil), that her Flag-Lieutenant, Mr. Coles, undertook the hazardous office of going in an open boat to the Bellerophon for assistance. The Rodney came about five to relieve, and the Agamemnon then engaged the Telegraph and Wasp Forts.

Whatever conclusion these facts may suggest as to the part played by the Fleets on the 17th, it appears that, in one respect, so favourable an opportunity as they then enjoyed, cannot recur. The Russians, taught by experience, are said to have deepened their embrasures in Fort Constantine, so as to admit of the guns being hereafter depressed to the requisite level.

But to get back to *terra firma*. Deserters bring very cheering accounts of the distress in

Sebastopol, and these appear to be confirmed
by the circumstance, that there is not more
than one man seen working every three or
four guns.   Our sharpshooters do excellent
service.   They brought in a Russian Officer
the other day, shot through both jaws with
a Minié ball; it had also cut the root of his
tongue so deeply as to make the end protrude
from his mouth; and there was the greatest
danger of his dying either from suffocation,
or from the impossibility of swallowing food.
He was placed in a little ruin used as a store-
house, and I lately went with ——, of Brigadier
General ——'s Staff, to ascertain if we could
be of use to him.   He never looked up as we
came in.   It was night, and it was piteous to
see him by the glimmering candle light in that
desolate place, sitting in his shirt on an old
box, before being put to bed; his face tied up,
and his swollen tongue being laved by the
soldier who attended him.   But my reason for
describing to you such misery is to come.
By the skill of Dr. Alexander, of the Light
Division, this man recovered sufficiently to be
sent on board ship; and he left the poor soldier
who had helped to clothe him out of his own

scanty wardrobe, and who had nursed him, like a woman, night and day — without a single look, sign, or token of acknowledgment!

The doctors have enough to do just now. Cholera is gone, but diarrhœa remains, and lying o' nights in the trenches is not good for the complaint. Still, though I often talk to the men out on picket, I never hear them grumbling; they only seem anxious to know when they are to storm "Sebastopool," and, 'faith, they are not singular in their curiosity.

I have just been thoroughly sickened by seeing poor ——, and ——, go off ill in one of those white hearses, called ambulances. Fancy a live man being put on a stretcher and slid into a kind of pigeon hole, under the seats, in the body of such a vehicle! I was glad that —— determined to sit out the journey, as he best might, on the bench. They are going on board ship at Balaklava, and till they return, the General will have but one Aide-de-camp.

LETTER VIII.

Camp, Oct. 29th.

WELL! I have seen a Battle, or rather part —
the bloodiest part — of a Battle; and am
amazed to find how little I have seen! If I
had been told beforehand, that the spectacle
of two armies, arrayed front to front in a
spacious valley, and assailing each other with
the deadliest instruments of modern warfare,
differs little, to the mere eye, from a Review
—that even to the *mind* of one "who hath
no friend or brother there," the Event of the
Day is so absorbing, that at the moment, he
hardly heeds the human wrecks, dwarfed
by distance into pigmies, which mark the
course of every manœuvre — that a single-
combat is more stirring than a general Engagement, and the anguish of one poor wounded
wretch, whose groans are in your ears, more
shocking than the most wholesale slaughter—
I should have doubted. Yet such is the les-
son of my own experience, and I believe that

those who have witnessed similar scenes would, if true to themselves, bear me out in the avowal.

I am glad, at any rate, that you do not depend upon me, exclusively, for an account of the Battle of Balaklava.   How any one, who has not somebody in the secrets of the Generals by his side, to explain the movements, can understand an affair of the kind, is to me a mystery.   If a man is in the *melée*, he sees only that.   If, on the other hand, he is at a sufficient distance to take in the whole field, he sees an array of dark sparkling masses — now moving, now stationary — covered with smoke, or emerging from it.   Finally, he sees a certain portion of the whole marching away, perhaps in very good order.   We will suppose that, at such a juncture, by good luck, he really does know that the fight is decided, and which party it is that is retreating; and that he rejoices, or laments, appropriately.   Nevertheless, as regards all the sudden emergencies, the daring movements, and sagacious plans — all, in fact, that give the battle its historical interest — our spectator comprehends no more of them, be-

lieve me, than you comprehend of the ma-
nœuvres of a Review.

And now, having reduced your anticipa-
tions to the proper level, let me fairly own, that
I was on the wrong side of the Ridge for observing the most interesting portions of the engagement of the 25th. The reason was, that when,
on that morning, repeated discharges of musketry and artillery in our rear proclaimed the
long-expected arrival of Osten-Sacken's force,
I, in common with my neighbours, believed
that it would very soon be beaten back again.
The enemy were advancing at the time towards the ridge to which I have alluded, and
which traversed the valley at a point between
them and Balaklava. Now, this ridge, though
a great deal lower than the hills which it
connects, is yet high enough to conceal from
persons on one side of it, the movements of
troops for some distance behind the other.
Assuming, therefore, that the enemy would
be routed and pursued, I determined not to
let the ridge intervene between me and the
sport, and took up my position on what
may be called the Russian, as opposed to
the Balaklava, side, at the French Mortar

Battery under the telegraph. The battery is situated just under the crest of the Western hill-side of the valley in the rear of our Camp, and commands a view of Balaklava to the right, broken only by the unlucky ridge. The valley must be a mile and a half broad. The hills are of limestone rock, rising steeply from the two sides of the plain, and are fantastically scarped, like most of the Crimean heights; while the general landscape, even in the valley, is just as brown, and sterile, as on the plateau. The whole country, in fact, looks as if it was made for fighting; but by no means as if it was worth fighting about.

On arriving at the battery about half-past eight, I could see the Russians (computed at 20,000 strong) defiling from behind some rising ground to our left, on the opposite, or Eastern, side of the valley. Numerous loose horsemen preceded them. Detached portions of the force were scattered over the whole breadth of the plain, and the mortars near which I stood, played upon some of the nearest of them with evident effect. We watched the shells bursting over and among them, and producing large gaps in their masses; but it was too far to see indi-

viduals being killed. The fire was not returned.

After half an hour or so had been thus
spent, a body of Russian horse charged over
the nearest end of the ridge, and to the great
mirth and delight of our party (I was standing among some French Officers) we soon
saw them galloping back again. Then they
joined the main body on the Eastern side
of the valley, and the whole advanced up
the farthest end of the ridge, where there
were three Turkish redoubts, giving a cheer
as they reached the summit. To our in-
tense chagrin, they stopped there. We saw
nothing like resistance. After a time, the
troops of the British First Division (who had
been ordered down from the camp) began to
cross the ridge about its centre, and bodies
of our cavalry took up their position between
them and the Western hills. The larger portion of the Russian force then retired half a
mile. Our troopers shortly afterwards were
seen galloping towards the enemy. There was
a mass of smoke; and when it cleared away,
we saw many corpses strewing the ground;
and some horses galloping riderless, and some

lying on the field. Whether they were British soldiers who had been slaughtered, or Russians, or both, we could not tell; but after the smoke had cleared away, the *melée* was at an end. Excepting some sharp firing behind the Balaklava side of the ridge, in the direction of the redoubts, we could discover or hear nothing more; till at two, becoming impatient, I went down to the ridge to an earthwork manned by a French regiment (the 27th). Here I perceived the whole arrangement of the British force. They were formed in three rows, extending across the valley; the first composed of regiments of the Line; the second of troopers standing by their horses; the third of the Guards and Highlanders. Ambulances were posted here and there; and everything seemed ready for a general action; but after waiting till four, and seeing no new symptoms of a move on either side, I returned to camp — there to learn what I had really been looking at!

I soon ascertained, that all the most effective portion of the battle had taken place on that side of the ridge which I had visited too late. The Russians whom we saw galloping back

over it in the morning, were no doubt th
relics of those whom the Heavies, as you wil
have learnt, had drubbed so heartily, an
against such fearful odds—one of the fe
spectacles in modern warfare, by the bye, which
from its having been a purely cavalry affair
had none of its effect marred by smoke. Th
splendid reception given by the 93rd High
landers to the Russian cavalry, was shut ou
from us by the same unlucky screen. Th
troopers whom we had watched dashing int
the fire of musketry and artillery on the furthe
side of the valley, were, it is true, then and ther
making their terrible charge under Lord Cardi
gan; but so dense was the pall in which the
were at once wrapped by the musketry and ar
tillery of the enemy—so complete, too, ou
ignorance of the nature and object of the move
ment—that even now I can hardly believ
myself to have witnessed that sublime displa
of military devotion. I had so far provide
against this annoyance by arranging with ——
that I was to accompany *him* in the event of an
engagement taking place, when I should hav
been pretty sure of seeing the best of every
thing, and with the best lights. But he, poo

fellow, was, and is, sick on board the ——;
and even had it been otherwise, I suppose his
duty would have compelled him to remain
behind in camp with his chief, to look after
the front. And—but that is enough in all
conscience! Why I should have told you so
long a story, with so little to tell, I'm sure I
don't know, unless to convince you that seeing a battle is not always comprehending it,
and to make you of a grateful and contented
mind with your newspaper in the Temple.

Next day I again went to the rear, and rode
pretty close to the two redoubts, which were
taken by the enemy, and which still remain
in their hands. Cavalry pickets were posted
near the other earthwork; but I learnt, that
no attempt would be made on the part of
the Allies to offer battle. Certainly, unless
some great advantage was to be gained by a
general engagement, one thing is enough at
a time, when that thing is the siege of Sebastopol; while there could be no point of honour
with the Western Powers in driving the enemy
from posts which were wrested only from Turks.

By the way, the misconduct of these rascals,
who, not content with running away, plun-

dered the tents of the Cavalry Division, will go far towards dispelling the pleasing illusion that prevails at home respecting their character. I was once told by Major ——, the best authority on the subject, that the far-famed defence of Silistria was due much more to Arnaouts and Egyptians than to the race who got all the credit of it. The common cry is, however, that Turks will do anything " if well officered." But no more formidable qualification of the assertion could be added. How are good Officers to be found for them? If, by way of encouraging bravery, recourse is had to the ranks, it is found that a commission is apt to nullify the very virtue it was meant to reward. The Turkish soldier transformed into an Officer, however valiantly he may have acquitted himself before, immediately resolves that, having won the things which make life pleasant, he will not further risk it. To quote an example that was lately mentioned to me; Latif Pasha was distinguished for daring as a private; he was rewarded by promotion, and ultimately obtained a brigade and the rank of Pasha; yet at Silistria, this quondam hero might at times be seen in tears at the head of his brigade; and poor Captain Butler was, on one occasion, compelled to threaten to shoot him in order to make him lead on the troops.

If, on the other hand, you resort to Christian nations for Officers, the revolting character of Turkish morals is found to be a barrier to any thing like that proper sympathy which should exist between the men and their leaders. "Give young Turks," say some, by way of meeting the difficulty, " a moral training, without meddling with their religion, and promote them." But though these advisers rightly assume that it is his defective *morale*, and not his Mussulman faith, that makes the Turk deficient in the proper qualities of an Officer; they seem to forget that it is only that defective *morale* which enables him to tolerate the vices of his men. Qualify him in one respect, and you disqualify him in another. Certainly, the nut is a hard one to crack; but I should not be surprised if, some day, the Greeks were to crack it.

I saw eight or ten Russians, and three or four horses, lying dead, on the slope, as I rode over the spot where the affair with the Heavy

Cavalry took place. The rest, I suppose, had been buried in the twenty-four hours that had elapsed in the interval. The corpses bore the number " 12 " on their buttons, wore fur-trimmed pelisses, and belonged, I believe, to a crack regiment that goes by the name of the " Weimar Hussars." Their feet had already been stripped by our men of boots and stockings; a practice invariably resorted to, partly on account of the value of the articles themselves, and partly from a belief that money is to be found concealed in them. I noticed that the features of these men had become so coarse from exposure, that they expressed little beyond a stern, sad endurance. Still, the " last enemy " had lent their faces a dignity which I have not seen in the countenances of their living countrymen; and the stark, white feet told eloquently of death. It felt strange to find, and leave, them there alone, scattered among the stones and thistles — and not a living soul to watch!

Being bound for Balaklava, where —— and —— were still sick on board a transport, previous to their removal to the ——, I rode *viâ* the tents of the Cavalry Division, and called on some of my old fellow-passen-

gers of the Royals. Captain —— regaled me
on a luncheon of devilled ration-biscuits and
candied fruits. You open your eyes, and so
did I, at the un-Crimean dainties. The fact is,
that some German has had the wit to freight a
vessel to Balaklava with English stores. Cigars
(smokeable ones) are now selling at thirty
shillings a pound; and during the week or two
that the cargo may remain unexhausted, I dare
say a good many comforts will be purchase-
able at equally moderate prices. Afterwards,
nothing of the kind, perhaps, will be obtainable
for love or money. The laws of political economy
do not seem to operate here in raising prices
in full proportion to the demand; and scarcity,
rather than dearness, is the inconvenience to
be dreaded. I can only account for it by supposing, that the traders, knowing that they are
admitted only on sufferance, fear to lose favour
with the authorities by driving quite such hard
bargains as the necessities of the Army might
otherwise enable them to do. Still the prices are
quite high enough to remunerate handsomely
any merchants who may have the sense to
seize the opportunity. For instance, the cigars
in question, being only just good enough for

a camp, and having paid no duty, are probably fetching the importer 50 per cent. profit.

I cantered back to the front by about three,
and was deposited at the tents by the summary
process of the mare rolling over with me. Finding, however, that the troops were out, I re-
mounted her, and went forward towards the
right. Here were two or three regiments lying
on the ground, and every sign of business,
except actual fighting. It turned out that a
sortie of some 8000 men on the Second Division
had just been repulsed. The Russians had in
the morning sung a *Te Deum* at Sebastopol over
the English guns taken from the Turks the
day before, and under the double influence of
religion and rum, had been gulled by their
leaders into the singularly illogical conclusion
of attempting to win similar trophies from
the English themselves. Possibly, even those
leaders were not aware, that the Guards had returned from Balaklava on the previous evening.
It was all over, however. In my quest of a
battle in the rear, I had missed a very brilliant
affair in the front. I met Lord Raglan, General Brown, and the whole Staff, together with
Sir Edmund Lyons, returning from the field,
as I went back to my tent.

LETTER IX.

YOU will guess from the heading of this letter that I have " raised the siege ; " and so far as bidding farewell to camp-life goes, I have done so. Work-time is come, and Othello's non-occupation is, or ought to be, gone!

Observe, however, that my commissariat was not exhausted. There was still enough greasy meat for three days ; and half a bottle of sherry, given me by a friend, remained to be drunk. Nevertheless, one or two causes had, I will own, combined to quicken my departure. So bleak a wind had set in on the 29th, after some oppressively hot weather, that I had been compelled to double my clothing, and even then, could not get warm. Above all, during two mortal nights, the luckless Economites, shivering, and bent on being off, broke my rest with low moans, interspersed with a sort of rattle, which he has the faculty of making with his teeth. It was in vain that the good-natured ·Doctor accompanied me at all sorts of hours to the "kennel," and that there, by the light of a candle held in my hat, we challenged the Ionian to swallow both pill and potion. He took them without demur! If he shammed, he did it bravely; but his grinders rattled on unwearied, or paused but for such intervals as made the recurring hubbub only the more destructive of sleep. When, therefore, on the 30th, he declared, for the third time that week, that he would decamp on the morrow, whether I did or not, I succumbed. My kit was soon sold, and the next day we trudged to Balaklava.

By the time we reached the harbour, I had contrived to get a headache, while John, on the contrary, had regained his full share of health and spirits. Never did I hear of a case where change from bad air to a worse produced so rapid a cure as in his. The mischief, however, was, that I could make no use of his recovered energies in effecting the only object I had in view, which was to get rowed out of harbour to the ———. Nobody, I should tell you, at Balaklava, has yet had the penetration to make his fortune by starting boats for hire. One, must, therefore, depend on the charity of such naval Officers as may chance to be going in one's own direction, and to have seats disengaged. The consequence is, that hosts of people are to be seen every day wandering up and down the quay, snuffing up garbage, and devouring their dear hearts, who would willingly give five shillings for a row of perhaps as many minutes. Of course, my Ionian might have applied to dozens of the said Officers before they would have listened to him. Nothing, therefore, was left for it but to undertake the work myself. And wander about I did, shouting first to this man-of-war's boat, and then to that, till, what with my headache, the cold, and the stench, I thought my campaign was likely to have a bad end. At last Captain —— took pity on me, and, though he could spare no boat to take me to the ——, kindly allowed me to pass the night on board his own renowned two-decker.

Do you know, I am inclined to think it is worth spending a month in camp, if only to appreciate the luxury of going to bed at the end of the time! It is true, that during my tent-life, I never once felt any hardship in sleeping booted and clothed; and that, for the

simple reason, that I always *did* sleep as soon
as I blew out the candle. But when, on
board the ——, I for the first time for nearly
four weeks, lay with the smooth fresh sheets
lapping around me, I knew, and tasted the
difference between that rude prosaic method
of tumbling out of every-day life into barren
unconsciousness, and being deliciously wooed,
lured, and coaxed into repose. I could not,
indeed, help coquetting with the thing, and
tried hard to keep awake awhile, that I might
have my fill of the sensation; but it might not
be! In a quarter of an hour, I was stupidly
oblivious — from all which, you will perceive,
it follows, that the more a man roughs it,
the more luxurious his tastes become.

I was too late to catch —— on his way to
Head-quarters, though I landed at nine. It
appears, he leaves his ship by these early
hours nearly every morning for the purpose of
riding to Lord Raglan's, and of conferring with
him on the requirements of the expedition.
However, I met him on the quay when he returned, and he immediately renewed the hospitable offer he made to me when I first landed
in the Crimea. I have now been here two days,

and what with the kindness I have received, and the novelty to me of the ways and customs on board a first-rate man-of-war, I have found much to enjoy.

Sailors have so much the advantage over soldiers during actual war, that, to a person fresh from witnessing the sufferings of the latter, it is difficult, without an effort of reason, to give the former credit for enduring anything. Then the tars are such jovial fellows. They do everything to music, and make work itself a kind of dance. There are four or five hundred of them at this moment hauling up a rope, with their feet tramping to the tune of Rory O'More. Why, it is regular "down the middle and up again!" No one who looked for an instant at their hearty good-humoured faces, could suppose that they felt the exercise as a toil.

In camp, where no fiddle was to be had, they used to time their steps in hauling up the guns, by making one of their number sing; and in the trenches, their animal spirits showed themselves in the most exuberant daring. Captain Lushington, I heard the other day, told some of them who had worked for several

hours at the Seaman's Battery, that they might
" now go and have a lark." They instantly
jumped on the parapets to have it *there!* At
that battery, indeed, it is with the greatest
difficulty that they are restrained from exposing themselves in this way every moment, as
nothing will content them but watching the
course of the balls as they fire them! There
is but one martial duty with which they cannot
be trusted, and that is to guard the casks of
ration-rum — the spirit invariably vanishes
under their care. *Apropos* of this little foible,
somebody suggested, in reply to a remark on
the difficulties of penetrating into Sebastopol,
— " Only put up a grog-shop on the other side,
and the sailors will find their way through!"

I am not going to attempt to describe
to you the good ship ——, but I will mention
a single thing that struck me as very cha-
racteristic of the wonderful order and finish
of a man-of-war. After having been cour-
teously shown over the whole vessel by one of
the Officers — from the great 64-pounders,
(between two of which my cot is swung) to the
operation-table, which always stands ready for
its bloody use—I was taken into the carpenter's

shop. It was so dark, that a light was necessary to exhibit it by. Here, at any rate, I thought the elaborate arrangements elsewhere displayed, were not likely to be exemplified. But I was wrong. The spirit of order had found scope even in the carpenter's nails. These were stuck in little holes made for the purpose in the side of the shop, and were so placed as to form national and patriotic mottoes, such as "God save the Queen," and Nelson's last signal. One has heard the phrase, " as neat as a pin," but here was a carpenter's shop as neat as a natal pincushion!

The damage sustained by the ship at the bombardment is nearly all repaired. I can see, however, plenty of scars. I hear that the missile which told most on her, so far as vibration was concerned, was a small water-rocket that hit her low down near the keel. The shock received was as great as if she had struck on a rock. Its violence was accounted for on the hypothesis, that the compression of the explosion outwards by the weight of water, had increased the force of the explosion against the timbers.

What a softening, inexpressible grace is lent to a man-of-war by the Middies! It is particularly striking after living in a camp exclusively composed of mature men. The Army has nothing corresponding to these pretty little fellows, who, with their rosy cheeks, resemble their mamas much more than they do the heroes they are one day to be. To meet them, too, in the midst of stern work; and with the knowledge, that it was but the other day, that the poor boys were ducking their curly heads, and laughing, amidst shot and shell; possibly, with about the same sense of adventure, as if it had been a game at snow-balls! Never dream of degeneracy in a land where mothers thus devote their offspring. Talk of Sparta—of Rome! England alone rocks her children on the wave, and War is the " wolf" which suckles them.

LETTER X.

"Caradoc," Nov. 10th.

I AM on my way home; but as this letter will reach you some days before I can follow it, I take the opportunity of sending you a rapid account of what I have seen since I last wrote. You know, of course, from other sources, that a tremendous battle has been fought, and *how* it was fought. I shall as usual, therefore, relate only what I witnessed myself.

We were at breakfast on board the ——, on Sunday the 5th, when indistinct sounds of heavy firing attracted our attention; and Captain —— mentioned, that he had noticed them ever since dawn. Of course, the gig was soon manned, and took a strong party ashore. —— got a pony, but most of us, myself included, were compelled to walk. After a mile or two, I was obliged to diverge from the rest, as I meant to go in the first instance to my old camp-quarters, there to borrow ——'s mare (he had got well again, and had returned to work), and to join him and the General on the field.

It was a seven-mile up-hill trudge. The occupation of the valley by the Russians had closed the shortest way (by the telegraph); and the nearest road, moistened by a Scotch mist, had been churned by ammunition-waggons and horses' hoofs into unctuous mud. When, therefore, I had climbed to the crest of the plateau, I cut across country. The fog prevented one's seeing far ahead, but the sharp reports of musketry, and the roar of artillery, were quite enough to mark the direction, even without the stream of French and English soldiers, bearing on their backs, and on stretchers, the wounded to the rear. I did not stop to question these men, but tried to read in their faces the fortune of the day. They all looked grave, and behaved with a silent, manly propriety, in good keeping with their sad office; but quite at variance with the stories one reads of the conduct of soldiers when relieved, as these were, from surveillance.

On arriving at the road which leads to my old quarters, I found it full of waggons carrying ammunition *to* the field, and wounded *from* it. But I was surprised to perceive, when at last (about one) I arrived, that my friend –

and a brother Aide, instead of being in the thick of the contest, were in camp. Their looks showed that something wrong had happened, and I soon heard, with great concern, that poor General —— had been badly wounded, and was then lying, faint from loss of blood, in what used to be my tent. A shell had also hurt, but not severely, ——'s knee. Both my friends were naturally absorbed in devising means for conveying their gallant chief to some place where he would be more fitly sheltered than under canvass. But they found time, in a few hurried words, to describe the carnage which they had witnessed, and pointed out the spot (easily visible from the tents) where the battle had raged the most fiercely.

No nag, of course, could now be lent me, nor was there any one whom I could join in the field. The fight, however, had become purely one of artillery; and the best point of view — as well as the safest — for seeing the practice on both sides, was some position opposite the centre of the line of fire. Having ascertained that a place called the Five-gun Battery (in reality the Right Lancaster Battery), answered to this description, I decided on going there — not,

however, till I had succeeded, amidst the
painful excitement around, in obtaining some
ration-biscuit ! I felt the incongruity of ask-
ing for food at such a moment. I would have
given anything to have been able to weather
the day without. But I had taken a long walk,
and (if not knocked on the head between
whiles, which I did not anticipate) should
have to take another. So, being famished, I
asked, and was satisfied. I record the fact, because it illustrates the humbling truth, that
hunger is as callous as Launce's cur.

The Five-gun Battery is between the Round
Tower and the tents of the Second Division.
It commands the best view I have obtained of
Sebastopol; and, now that the fog had cleared
away, the city appeared to great advantage.
There was a mound behind the battery, four or
five feet high, so situated as to conceal persons
lying down under it, from the Russians in the
field, but not from the garrison in the town.
Nor was it quite steep enough, I should think,
to have stopped a rolling round shot from any
direction. Though, however, both the enemy's
field artillery on our right, and the fort and
ship guns on our left, commanded the position,

our party was too small to be much noticed. It consisted of General England and his Staff, and a troop of horse artillery. The horses of the latter, which the mound could not conceal, were probably the occasion of the very few missiles that actually lit near us. The Round Tower was firing over our heads at the Allied armies. The Russian park of artillery, on the other hand, had enough to do with the antagonists before them, who, already (it was not quite two o'clock) were slowly gaining ground. In fact, the only narrow escape I had, was from a shell, which did me the honour to burst within a few yards of me, when my ears were, foi the first and last time, regaled with the peculiar *hum* which marks the near approach of the flying fragments of those uncomfortable projectiles (I picked up a hot bit as a memento). Still, though we were comparatively safe, I was amused, considering all things, by the politeness of an Officer present, who on lighting his cigar from mine, expressed an artistic regret, that he should " spoil so beautiful an ash !"

At this time, the aspect of the battle, as seen from our position, was as follows. Two large bodies of the Allied troops stood, or rather lay, close before the foremost tents of the Second Division, a little below the long low rounded outline of the hill on which these are pitched, and which, on its furthest side, descends to the Tchernaya. Another mass occupied a place (as seemed to me) about a hundred yards in advance, on the very profile of the hill. The whole of this ground, I should tell you, rises gradually, for two or three hundred yards in front of the tents. Crossing the highest portion of its outline, was a fourth body of the Allies. The ground then makes a dip for about four hundred yards, when it makes another gradual rise of the same rounded character, until it reaches an elevation somewhat higher than the hill occupied by the French and British troops. Here I counted six bodies of the enemy. I suppose the two Armies were seven or eight hundred yards apart. All parties were pounding away with their artillery, and the wind carried off the smoke, so that we could clearly see the spectacle. About three, the Allied troops gradually advanced, till their foremost park of artillery occupied the bottom of the valley between the two hills. In half an hour more, the Russians were in full retreat towards Sebastopol. I could see them in their long grey coats marching past us, with their arms shouldered, and in good order.

My sketch of the ground was now completed, the victory won, and I got up and prepared for my long trudge, so as to be in time for dinner on board the ——; but I had not walked many paces, when one of our regiments was brought forward past me, to fire at the retreating foe. Stretchers were being carried behind them ; and though I had often seen such implements used in carrying the wounded, I confess, it gave me a shock to see them borne close behind these soldiers—now walking well and erect, their faces full in my view — *in anticipation!* An anticipation soon realised. Directly they arrived at the place where I had been lying, it seemed alive with round shot throwing up the dust in all directions; while the stretcher-bearers were running here and there—I knew too well for what reason.

It did also occur to me (why will thoughts cross one at the wrong times ?) that, perhaps, it was lucky for a certain person that these poor fellows did not come up before — that had

that happened, he might have presented himself at a particular nook of the Temple with
a wooden leg; but with no honours, no pension,
to show for it — only sharp shafts of ridi-
cule, and — "*Que, diable, allait-il faire dans
cette galère?*"   Ah, ha! you have lost that
triumph!

But to return — a very long way—the Lancaster gun in front is said to have done good service at this juncture, by mauling the retreating
columns of the enemy. I confess I looked hard
with my glass, and could see no gaps made,
nor any approach to unsteadiness. That,
however, proves nothing; as a battle is such a
huge complicated affair, and there is so much
difficulty in getting a full view of it, that it is
only by comparing the accounts of a large
number of witnesses, that a correct notion of
the whole can be obtained by anyone.

As I had to return in time for ——'s dinner,
I could not, as some of my friends did, go over
the field that evening. It was dark when I
got to Balaklava, and, as usual, a boat was
not to be had for love or money. A *deus ex
machinâ*, however, at length appeared, in no
less a person than Admiral ——, who kindly
gave me a seat in his gig. His Turks rowed

so well, that my contempt for the tribe was in complete abeyance, till I got on board the ——.

Here, I was rejoiced to learn, that the General had been safely brought. His cot was swung between two great guns, with a curtain drawn before it, in the cabin where we dined. Every one was glad, when, during our dinner, he rallied from his loss of blood sufficiently to put in, now and then, a word from behind his screen. He was lying in the cot I had myself slept in up to that day. Is it not a curious string of coincidences, that, when wounded on the field, he was given to drink some weak brandy and water, which I had mixed for the purpose of giving the wounded at Balaklava (the flask being part of the kit I had sold to one of his Aides) — that he was, next, put upon the stretcher, and in the tent, that had belonged to me — and that he was now lying in the cot which I had occupied?

When I left, he was well enough to walk about the cabin; making, in fact, rather too little of his wound. *Apropos* of his spirits in spite of it, I can't resist telling you a story. I dare say you know that he, like our gallant host, belongs altogether to the hopeful faction.

The first day that he was well enough to come to table, somebody (I forget who) happened to be talking very lugubriously about various things and the campaign in particular, and at length exclaimed, "Ah, war is a terrible thing!" "That's what my wife says," cheerily put in the General, and settled the croaker!

In England, one reads a good deal of plausible writing about the necessity for young blood in our military chiefs; and there is a *mot* on the subject attributed to the late Sir Charles Napier, which is certainly piquant. He was asked what he thought of the Army and Navy Club? "Fine young men—very!" What of the Junior United Service? "Fine *old* men — very !!" What of the Senior United Service? "Fine old *women—very!!!*" *A priori*, the young, at any rate, are apt to jump to the same conclusion. But observe, the sexagenarian himself had lost none of his dash and spirit, when he uttered the epigram. And whatever truth it may contain for greybeards in general, there are assuredly some among our veterans in the Crimea, of whom no one in his senses will believe, that, "in their hot youth," they could have possessed more glorious energy than they now display whenever " deeds of dering-do " are to be done. Whether their bodily frames will enable them to hold out against any long continuation of the hardships they are undergoing, is another matter.

The morning after the fight, I again walked to the front, and went over a portion of the field. No English wounded, I rejoice to say, were visible. I made many inquiries of the stretcher-bearers, while they were engaged in picking up those Russians who had lived through the night, and from what they told me, I infer that all, or nearly all, our poor countrymen were removed the evening before.

The slope on the other side of the tents is not very steep : in fact, a pony which I had borrowed in camp, walked up and down it quite easily. There was a good deal of low oak scrub, but it was not thick enough to prevent one's picking one's way through the place. Our men were digging large pits for burying the dead. The horrors I had heard of as having been witnessed on the field by those who went there directly after the action, were to a great degree abated. The Russians who yet survived, were too faint to do more than groan faintly. They seemed grateful, poor fellows, when I gave them small portions of brandy from my flask; but, as I had not tempered it with water, and wished to distribute it as widely as possible, I poured out only a tablespoonful for each man. It might, perhaps, have served to keep them alive, after the cold night, till they could be taken to hospital.

I could see comparatively few English and French among the dead. The former, as you know, fought in their grey great coats, from there not having been time to take them off; and the inconvenience which this occasioned, by confounding friend and foe, will, I should think, cut short the clamour against the hue of our Line uniforms. Those writers at home who have been running at red, like mad bulls, ignore the circumstance, that the French — pretty good judges in such matters — make their infantry wear trousers of the same colour. No doubt, it is an inconvenience for troops to be seen plainly by the enemy; but it is a greater one, not to be seen plainly by their own comrades; especially when, as happens in our case, the latter shoot the best of the two.

Many of the Russian dead had been stripped, and appeared to be good specimens of men. Most of them had blue eyes, regular features, coarse brown complexions, and averaged, I should say, rather more than the height of Frenchmen. They were provided with what looked like little bolsters, but which were really bags of crumbled brown biscuit. It did not taste bad, and, I suppose, it is given them broken up, for the purpose of being made more readily into porridge. Each man had four days' provisions; a circumstance which, with the fact of their having brought gabions and fascines, shows how confidently they expected to establish themselves on Sir De Lacy Evans's position.

The attitudes of the dead were most startling. I think I told you, that I found the Hussars, who were sabred by our Heavy Dragoons at Balaklava, lying flat on the ground. Here, on the contrary (and the same is said to have been the case at the Alma), the dead were strewed about in every imaginable posture. Arms were stretched upwards, as if warding blows, or dealing thrusts. Bodies were half raised—the head bent forward—the nether lip bit in—the eyes open—but for the glassy stare and marble feet, you might have thought them springing at your throat! The suddenness of the stroke had fixed the last movement of volition. Those who had bled to death, lay placidly.

You will have heard of the atrocities committed by the enemy on the wounded. As I returned from the field, I met two or three hundred prisoners being taken into Balaklava, upon whom, as they passed, all kinds of abuse were being lavished by our men. I saw one of these Russians, in particular, signalise a private who was smoking, to give him a light; but it was refused, with the most hearty maledictions. Now, as vindictive feeling towards the conquered is the very last sentiment that enters the breast of an English soldier, these are symptoms of the extent to which the barbarities in question are beginning to inflame the minds of our Army. Let the irritation go on a little longer, and "quarter" will be unknown.

During the whole course of my walk from the camp to the harbour, English and French Officers were making inquiries of me, respecting the health of the General.

On the 8th I obtained, by Captain Derriman's kindness, a passage in the vessel from which this is dated. She is bound for Constantinople, whence — as I have not time to deliver my letters at the Embassy — I shall proceed at once to England. Dining on board her, before she started, were the Duke of Cambridge and his Staff, General Bentinck (wounded in the arm), Major Nasmyth, and others. H. R. H. mentioned many interesting circumstances connected with Inkerman, and told us that a ball had penetrated his overcoat, but had glanced off, in consequence of striking against a gold cuff-button of his shirt. He was suffering from aguish symptoms, but looked well, considering the amount of rough work which he had gone through.

About nine P.M., I saw my last of the ———. On board her were all those to whom chiefly it was due, that my visit to the Crimea was an enjoyable one.

THE END.

A. and G. A. SPOTTISWOODE,
New-street-Square.